Acknowledgements

First and foremost, we would like to acknowledge and thank all of the personnel that were involved in this incident. You are to be admired for your dedication and diligence when called upon to participate in the successful outcome of peaceful resolution in the Morey Tower Takeover.

Special thanks go to Jennifer Hogansen, Ph.D., Psychologist, for her insight and guidance during the development of this book and also to Mike Hogansen for his literary input and editing.

Thanks to Correctional Lieutenant Charles Hughes for his expertise, leadership, and guidance in continuing to provide advice, both professionally and personally, that has proven invaluable in the completion of this book.

We also would like to recognize Jennifer Hurad from rightshadeofwow.com for her creation of an amazing book cover in a timely manner. And thank you Tanya and Dodie in Walla Walla for your efforts and time, and also to Mark Thibault for his input.

Special thanks go out to a young journalism student named Hayden, who's input and efforts to make this noteworthy account accurate and credible are very much appreciated. Also thanks go out to Gene in Oregon for setting the format.

We would like to recognize Steve Robertson and Correctional Lieutenant Bruce Frank, Crisis Response Negotiators, for their research, knowledge, and insight into the new field of Profiling Internal Behaviors.

We would like to also acknowledge Lee B. Rose in Walla Walla for his years of support with this project.

"I've got nothing to lose, and this is an escape! If you do what I tell you, nobody will get hurt!"

"You better say the right thing mother-fucker, or I'll stab you in your fucking head."

"Lois, You ready to die?"
"I've been ready to die since the day that you came in here."

"You're dying first. Are you ready to die?"
"Can I ask one thing, if....before you shoot me?"
"What???"
"Shoot me in the head. Make it quick."

HOSTAGE

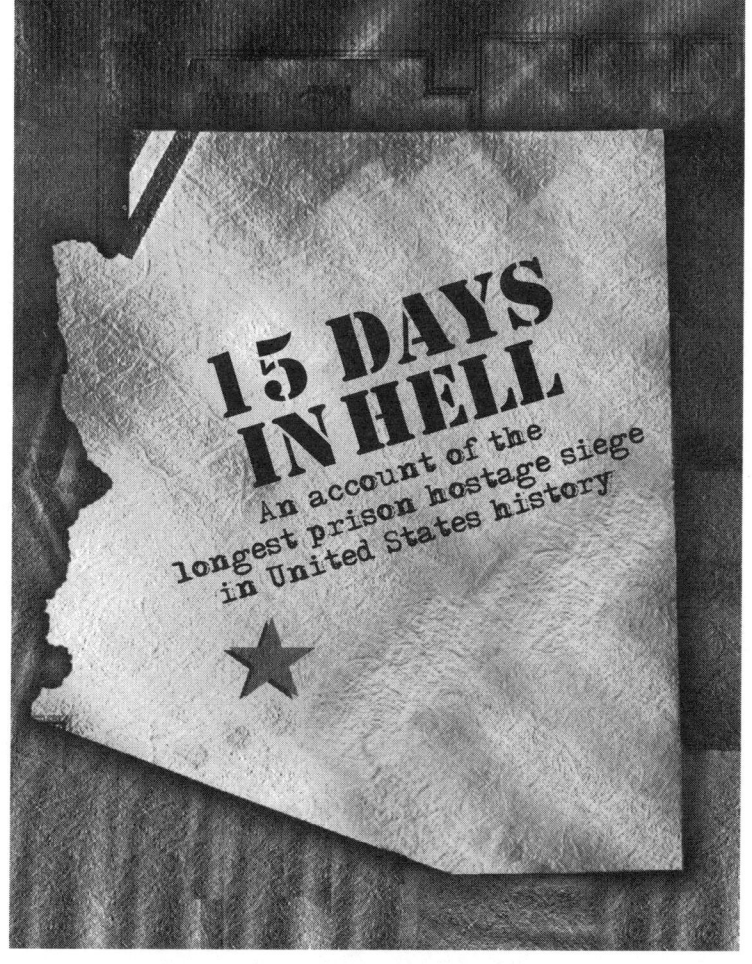

15 DAYS IN HELL
An account of the longest prison hostage siege in United States history

Keith Rapp and Robert Davis

All rights reserved
Copyright Keith Rapp and Robert Davis 2006
Printed in the United States of America
By www.PrintmediaBooks.com

ISBN-10: 0-9790999-8-6
ISBN-13: 978-0-9790999-8-4

Foreword

A good friend of mine recently commented, "I think that Lois Fraley is a Guardian Angel. Everybody's life she touches benefits somehow from knowing her." That good friend is Robert "Bob" Davis, the Chairman and co-founder of the The Lois Fraley Foundation, a 501 (c) (3) non-profit organization that is dedicated to serving others with what The Survivor Lois Fraley has learned first hand by enduring the longest prison hostage siege in United States history.

As a Crisis Negotiator and an Instructor in Hostage Survival with the Washington State Department of Corrections, I was affected deeply, although peripherally by Lois Fraley's critical incident spanning fifteen days in the early months of 2004. As I researched this incident, reviewing thousands of pages of documents and recordings, it was my intention to build a vehicle that would "drive home" the message that Hostage Survival training is a necessity, as well as an obligation that should be provided to line staff by their high risk employers; Jail and Prison Systems, Banks, Airlines, Hospitals, School Systems and Community Mental Health Agencies.

As I digested Officer Fraley's Fifteen Days in Hell, I became deeply interested in knowing what the dynamics were that contributed to this nightmarish event being resolved peacefully through negotiations. But, more important to me was to understand and to learn how this woman, who I consider to be an icon in the fairly new world of hostage survival, did what she did; she came out alive.

Through her emotional and spiritual journey, the Guardian Angel that is Lois has allowed me to become something that I wasn't before, a dedicated writer. Because of my interest and the interest of my peers, I began researching and writing about the "Lewis Prison Tower Takeover." Over the last two years I have generated thousands of pages of text, documenting the entire incident from a myriad of different views; a negotiator's, as well as a former tactical team member's perspective, along with the voices and perspectives of those who were actually involved in the incident. My account is based solely on information that was released publicly by law enforcement, news sources and the transcripts of actual interviews conducted during The Governor's Blue Ribbon Panel along with that panel's after report titled, "Preliminary Findings and Recommendations: The Morey Unit Hostage Incident."

My Guardian Angel has taken me even further by changing my profession from Corrections to Consulting. This woman's influence and story caused me to reassess my own life after I became involved in two bloody critical incidents within weeks of each other in October of 2005 at the Washington State Penitentiary in Walla Walla.

From Lois' crucial ordeal, my own life has been transformed and taken on a new meaning. In 2006, after seventeen years of service, I left the Department of Corrections to create a training and consulting business, "Survival Resources" with the intention of "Teaching Valuable Lessons for Critical Incident Survival." Out of respect for Lois and the necessary healing that I knew was ahead of her, I remained an outside observer as I followed the trials and the unpredictable antics of Ricky Wassenaar and Steven Coy.

Finally, after two years, I reached out to the Lois Fraley Foundation by emailing a short message. From this outreach I offered my services, and became a consultant to the Foundation.

This re-creation of Lois Fraley's Fifteen Days in Hell is authenticated emotionally by Robert Davis, who has provided me with profound insights into this national incident that were gleaned from his close relationship and hundreds of hours of conversations with Lois herself.

It is our hope that you will find this important story to be of interest, and that by reading it you, in turn, will also gain some beneficial knowledge of the different phases of a hostage incident and the human dynamics that are an integral part of the negotiations process.

The proceeds of this book will help the Lois Fraley Foundation to achieve its worthwhile goals by helping those in need, and educating others.

Keith Rapp
Instructor/Consultant
Survival Resources
www.survivalresources.org

Table of Contents

Prologue ix

Chapter One
O Dark 30..1

Chapter Two
This is an Escape! 9

Chapter Three
Fresh Air 13

Chapter Four
15 Days in Hell Begins 27

Chapter Five
Raped and Rescued 31

Chapter Six
Shoot to Kill 41

Chapter Seven
Death, Surrender or Rescue? 49

Chapter Eight
Suicide by Cop 57

Chapter Nine
Finger for Food 65

Chapter Ten
A Long Night for Lois 77

Chapter Eleven
Left Behind 81

Chapter Twelve
Divide and Conquer 91

Chapter Thirteen
The Teams 101

Chapter Fourteen
The Suits 109

Chapter Fifteen
Just Another Day 127

Chapter Sixteen
Lois' Super Sunday 139

Afterword 155

Glossary 161

Bibliography 167

About the Writers 169

Prologue

In the middle of an isolated Southwest desert sits the Arizona Prison Complex-Lewis, the state's largest penitentiary, boasting a population of over 4,100 convicted felons.

The institution, which is on Day Nine of an emergency "lockdown," is illuminated by the morning's dawn and the bright lights that sit atop numerous tall poles. The lights of satellite television broadcasting trucks add to the glow, while a wide variety of emergency lamps flash different colors and rhythms.

The sounds of diesel generators run above the radio dialogue blaring from the variety of vehicles that are on-site with their staff. Present are police officers, ambulance attendants and firefighters. A SWAT armored personnel vehicle sits loaded with team members garbed in black tactical gear.

Across the highway in a press staging area, tripod mounted cameras with telephoto lenses whir while their shutters click, as isolated photographers attempt to record the incident for the evening news.

In front of one of the news trucks, a female reporter stands confidently in a modern suit and stylish jacket holding a microphone, not yet in use. She is in her early thirties but has the appearance of a younger woman; her auburn hair is coiffed to shoulder length adding to her commanding appearance.

Lisa is speaking to someone off-camera as she looks into a nearby monitor, "Do we have the dual feed yet?" When camera lights come on suddenly, the journalist raises her microphone; she is on the air.

"Good Morning Phoenix, this is Lisa Volenec, KNXV Channel 15 News, reporting live from the Arizona State Prison Complex-Lewis, on this, Day Nine, of the 'Lewis Tower Takeover,' which is rapidly approaching the longest hostage taking in US prison history."

Inside of The Morey Unit Guard Tower, Correctional Officer Lois Fraley is shackled in place listening to a small AM/FM radio reporting the story of her plight, her only means of connection with the outside world.

The Hostage, who sits on the floor of the filthy tower, is clad only in her dirty and bloodied uniform shirt and prison issued men's orange underwear.

Carcasses of hundreds of dead flies are revealed by the morning sun passing through the peepholes cut into ceiling tiles that are used to black-out the windows. The shafts of light illuminate dust motes as they float lazily in the still air. Lois does not look good, she is sweating; her disheveled, matted hair surrounds her dirty, gaunt face.

Lois' wrists are handcuffed in front of her and are attached to a chain that is secured to the floor of The Tower. The hostage listens in earnest, sobbing dirty tears as a radio broadcast continues, "These must indeed be the longest days in the life of Lois Fraley, the 33 year-old correctional officer and single mother being held against her will in The Tower by two desperate convicts, armed with assault rifles and shotguns."

As flies buzz throughout the stale air of The Tower, Lois struggles with her manacled hands to scratch a ninth hash mark below one of the blacked out window's sills with a small pencil stub.

Across the room, a large tattooed hostage taker snores as he sleeps upright, cradling a shotgun. Coy is muscular with tattoos of snakes from shoulders to wrists and his once clean shaven head and beard now show signs of stubble.

Standing in the crisp desert morning's air Lisa looks into a video monitor as she continues to report from the remote location, "It was nine days ago today that Ricky K. Wassenaar and Steven John Coy captured The Tower and its arsenal, as well as two Correctional Officers; Lois Fraley and Jason Auch."

Many miles away, across the large expanse of Phoenix, a wall-mounted television set plays Lisa's newscast while Jason Auch, with his face and head bandaged, lies in a hospital bed, attached to IVs and other medical equipment. The young man is being attended to by a nurse and a doctor while a uniformed police officer stands guard at the door.

On the television's screen, several different images of Jason and Lois are displayed. The injured young man watches in earnest as the background pictures change from Lois and him to distant views of The Tower from various angles and lenses.

A tear runs down Jason's face while he watches an earlier news clip showing him being loaded from a gurney onto a helicopter.

Lisa Volenec continues, "Jason Auch, who was severely injured during the assault on The Tower remains in serious condition."

Images play of Ricky Wassenaar dressed in an officer's uniform walking on top of The Tower's observation deck defiantly smoking a cigarette. On nearby roof tops snipers and spotters are seen lying in their "hides" observing the rebellious hostage taker.

The newswoman reports," We will continue to update our viewers throughout the day, or as significant changes occur. Prison staffs throughout the state are expressing solidarity for the kidnapped officer and her family while concerned citizens raise money as well as support."

Inside of The Tower, Lois listens to the small radio as she looks down at the two small tattered photographs clasped in her grubby hands.

Lois begins to pray silently, her lips moving and eyes closed, as she continues to listen to her own story. "It all began in the early morning of January 18th."

Chapter One
0 Dark 30

January 18, 2004 started off as normal as a day can for the people who work their jobs during what is affectionately known as "0Dark30." On this particular January morning, Tower Officer Lois Fraley is working the "graveyard" shift with her newest co-worker, Officer Jason Auch. Graveyard is a ten-hour shift that runs from 2040 hours, military time, (8:40 PM) until 0640 hours, (6:40 AM) with 0Dark30 falling somewhere in between.

Lois is a solid woman who hails from Shreveport, Louisiana, something that becomes obvious once you've spoken with her. The 33 year-old single mother's brown hair is worn short in a way that many women now like to wear it, adding to her look of self-assurance that carries her large frame and proportional figure with confidence. She is a pleasant woman and a dedicated parent to her twelve-year-old daughter, Kyla. But tonight, she is not a mother; she is a mentor for Jason, whose inexperience to corrections brings with it a certain naive excitement.

Jason Auch is 21 years-old and definitely considered to be a "fish," prison slang accepted by both inmates and officers alike, for "the new guy." He is working at a level of conscious incompetence; basically, he knows what he doesn't know. Jason realizes that he has a lot to learn and, so far, has enjoyed working The Tower and learning from Officer Fraley.

Jason has heard Lois described as an excellent backup when the *shit hits the fan*. She is definitely not what one would call dainty, and can be quite outspoken. Officer

Fraley's level of job experience makes her unconsciously competent; she can do the job without thinking. Her years in corrections have not only taught Lois what to do, but also what not to do.

As the morning becomes a new day, Lois and Jason have no idea just how wild things are going to get. By the time this day is over there will have been physical and mental assaults, stabbings, rapes and gun battles. A young man will have his new dreams crushed, while a woman named Lois Fraley will begin a journey of survival with no idea to what extent her spirit will be tested over the next fifteen days.

The Arizona State Prison Complex-Lewis is in the middle of nowhere and close to nothing. This 330 acre facility is so remote that correctional staff receive an additional 15 percent pay just for working there. The maximum-security prison is thirty-seven miles south of Phoenix and thirteen miles "just this side" of the small desert community of Buckeye, Arizona, population 6,500.

But that number does not include the 4,100 men who have been banished to live in this desert prison. These are the offenders that society and the courts of the State of Arizona have deemed inappropriate to live among us. These are the drug dealers, the thieves, the rapists, the child molesters and the murderers that decent people and politicians want removed from our streets.

Locked inside the confines of the prison's Morey Unit, Ricky Wassenaar and Steven Coy are two such habitual offenders. For years they have been planning an escape with only one goal in mind, freedom. And if escape isn't possible, they might as well die trying because neither one of these hardcore convicts would want to fail and live with defeat. But who are they, and how did they get to where they are on this critical January morning in the desert?

Ricky Kurt Wassenaar, a.k.a. "Rooster," is known to the

Arizona Department of Corrections as Inmate #065155. He is 41-years-old and has been diagnosed as an anti-social living within our society. He is manipulative, egotistical, narcissistic and has earned a reputation in prison parlance as a "Jail House Lawyer" or "Legal Beagle." Wassenaar also has quite the reputation as a hard-line gambler with the infractions history to prove it. Infractions in prison are rule violations that are usually punished with periods of isolation. Wassenaar is currently serving a sentence of twenty-eight years in prison for armed robbery and assault, his earliest possible release date is February of 2022.

Steven Michael Coy, a.k.a. "Pony," is Inmate #047122. He is 40-years-old and also feels that obeying the rules of society is not his responsibility. But, unlike Wassenaar, Coy is not even a good criminal. At best, he is an inadequate personality-type whose addiction and obsession with sex has landed him in prison for the rest of his natural life. This is the low-life that conned his pregnant girlfriend into driving a getaway car during their robbery of a Tucson business in 1993. He was apprehended, prosecuted and sentenced as a result of deciding to stick around the scene of the crime to rape the business owner. Coy is currently serving seven consecutive life sentences with his earliest possible release date in February of 2076.

Rooster and Pony are cell mates, or as convicts call themselves "cellies," and have been planning an escape for a long time. These felons have exhausted the appeals process and court system as a remedy for their confinement, and have what they consider a well calculated plan that was set in motion shortly after Coy was returned to the prison's Protective Segregation Unit (PSU) after serving a sanction of six weeks in the "hole" for attempting an escape with a weapon. The hole is the jail within the prison where disciplinary sanctions are served in isolation cells. The sanctions are given for a variety of offenses ranging from lying to murder.

Wassenaar, the brains of this motley outfit, works as a cook in the Morey Unit kitchen where he has been studying the weaknesses in the prison's security practices for four years. He has chosen a Sunday graveyard shift to launch his plan; he knows that at this early hour the unit is vulnerable, mostly guarded by "fish."

It should be noted that during this critical incident only one of the officers involved had more than sixteen months of experience at the Morey Unit complex.

The high number of "fish" on duty can be explained by the fact that in the Arizona Department of Corrections (ADC), 697 correctional officers resigned their positions in 2002 alone. The Arizona Prison Complex-Lewis holds the record for the highest loss rate in the entire state, at 27.2 percent. Dora Schriro (Director of the Arizona State Department of Corrections) spoke about the Lewis Complex saying that it has a disproportionately large number of "junior staff," the breadth and depth of service is just not there.

What lies ahead for these two convicts who are hell bent on escape? Wassenaar and Coy are about to take two correctional officers, as well as the entire State of Arizona Department of Corrections captive, in what will eventually become the longest prison hostage siege in United States history.

Their plan is to escape to Vermont. If Ricky K. Wassenaar and Steven John Coy can reach the arsenal stored within The Tower, freedom is just a mad dash away. If these two hardened convicts can persuade others to join them in the escape, all the better.

During a radio interview Wassenaar explained:
"The prison has reported it as an escape attempt based solely on what I told them. I was working on the plan since I arrived there in 2000." Wassenaar continued with little

emotion, *"Everything was calculated, although the timing got screwed up right from the start."*

It sure did. Ricky Wassenaar will have many days to think about that fact and to thank Steven Coy for being trapped by who they refer to as the "pigs." Once again, it was Coy's proclivity for sexual assault that ruined this escape attempt for himself and his partner in crime.

Another of the early morning people is Civilian Kitchen Worker Rosa Garcia, a pseudonym used to protect her identity, aged sixty-three. Rosa has worked at the prison for a while now in a job that she really doesn't mind, although today she does not feel well. She supervises maximum security inmates in their daily toils of producing enough food for the men who have been sentenced to this prison in the desert.

After discussing with her husband whether or not to go to work at all, she decided to go to the prison so that there would be two civilian workers on duty in the kitchen. When Rosa arrived at work a little after 2:00 AM, she realized that she was the only one there, so she went into the kitchen's office and began to fill out paperwork.

At the same time in a cell within the Morey Housing Unit, Ricky Wassenaar prepares for his duties in the kitchen where he will work for Rosa and a new civilian kitchen worker named James. Wassenaar's work in the kitchen may actually begin later that morning, but his underhanded work on James began weeks ago.

Ricky stands at the cell's steel sink brushing his teeth. He wears immaculate orange kitchen worker clothing that he launders himself. He is a fastidious man who is known by many as a Type-A personality. The convict stands a trim 5'9" and sports a winter's growth of a well manicured beard that covers his thin lips and acne scarred face. His winter beard is a yearly ritual that the guards have come to accept. If only correctional staff knew that along with

James, this well-groomed beard is also a part of Ricky's ingenious escape plan.

Steven Coy lies in the cell's upper bunk dressed in his stain-covered kitchen uniform. His build is short and stocky with his shaved head sitting atop a large tattooed neck. He is propped on his bunk, looking at a porno magazine. When the cell door opens, Coy hides the magazine beneath his mattress and exits with his "cellie."

At approximately 0200 hours outside of the Morey Living Unit, tired prisoners, known to officers as 10-15s, deal with the tedium of confinement as they assemble waiting for an escort to the kitchen. This is all just a part of the daily ritual that is known as prison life. Like being in the military, the convicts are expected to "hurry up and wait" to be pat searched by unit staff checking them for weapons.

While waiting their turns, Wassenaar and his soon-to-be barricaded partner discuss their plan with hushed tones. They abruptly stop talking when the two escorting correctional officers (C/Os); Coy Kelley and Elizabeth Debaugh arrive. The bearded Ricky is attentive as Kelley speaks into his radio.

"Is it clear to move the 10-15s to the kitchen?"

Over Kelley's radio, Lois Fraley's southern drawl is heard, "10-4 the Yard is clear."

Ricky smiles as he intently listens to the radio call and response. He then whispers to his partner "You ready to do this?"

Coy replies, "Since the day I was born, Rooster. You got this thing down?"

Ricky is incredulous. "Man, four years of checkin' this shit out? Yeah, I got it down; it's a no-brainer. Ain't nothin' but 'fish' working on this shift."

Coy looks at Wassenaar with genuine admiration and then asks him the question, "You think this will work?"

Ricky responds, "Hell yeah. Once we get into that

tower, we've got the guns and the way out. We 'hot foot' it on up to the Admin Building, and we're outta this shithole."

Coy and Wassenaar begin to walk with the fifteen other inmates through the "Blue Yard" towards the Morey Unit kitchen door. The "Blue Yard" which allows access to the kitchen entrance is one of two, of the Morey Unit recreation yards, the other being the "Red Yard."

Meanwhile, in the Morey Unit kitchen, Rosa walks with Officer Martin, the unit's only C/O who works the graveyard shift. He receives a radio transmission asking him to unlock the kitchen door, allowing direct access to the incoming inmate workers. The officer suddenly remembers an earlier phone call and comments, "By the way Rosa, James isn't coming in today. He called in sick."

The woman asks, "Why does that not surprise me?"

Her sarcastic remark is met with a look of understanding.

James is the newest civilian employee for CANTEEN, the private contractor that feeds Arizona Department of Corrections inmates. It is later believed that his absence from work this morning is a secret sign to Wassenaar and Coy to go ahead with their escape. It is also believed, but has not been substantiated, that James may be responsible for providing the materials and the hiding places for two makeshift knives, as well as for Wassenaar's electric razor which is concealed somewhere within the kitchen.

After settling in and donning their hair nets, the inmate kitchen crew begins to prepare pancakes for the morning meal. While walking through the kitchen Rosa is approached by Wassenaar who asks, "Ma'am, is James here?"

She responds evasively, "I don't know, he might come in later, he's not here right now."

Pleased with the deceptive answer, Wassenaar grins and then enters a large walk-in refrigerator carrying a 30-inch stainless steel paddle used for stirring pancake batter. Coy, who follows, walks directly towards the back of the cooler to retrieve two large prison-made knives from a plastic case that holds individual milk cartons.

In prison, homemade knives are known as "shanks" or "shivs." Their purpose is to allow an inmate a feeling of security or, in this case, dominance. The officers at the Arizona Prison Complex-Lewis have observed a wide variety of shanks in both quality and lethality. But these two particular weapons are notable examples of what are also known as "pig stickers."

ADC staff witness inmates trying to kill each other every day and, my God, do they get close. Correctional officers don't want to see a man's throat laid open by a razor blade melted into a toothbrush, a throat cut so deeply that it is necessary to lay a gloved hand into the neck up to the third knuckle to keep the victim from bleeding out.

They have run with many a gurney to the Trauma Room at the Arizona Prison Complex-Lewis and they've ridden to hospitals in the back of the ambulances being followed by armed officers in the chase cars while their charges lay bleeding or dying from some self-induced or group-induced violence. They've cut down the hangers and they've strapped down the cutters to save the lives of men who want to die. But, sometimes it is too late. It's not unusual to go home and say to a family member, "I saw a dead guy today."

Chapter Two
This is an Escape!

In the kitchen's office, Rosa is seated at a desk looking down when the two convicts burst through the door wielding their weapons. Wassenaar rushes towards Martin brandishing the stirring paddle in one hand and a 10-inch shank in the other. Coy also hovers over the male officer, menacing him with the second large shank.

Wassenaar boldly makes his announcement, "I've got nothing to lose and this is an escape! If you do what I tell you, nobody will get hurt!"

As the terrified woman cowers, Martin is subdued and intimidated by Coy who removes the guard's two-way radio from its holster on his belt.

Ricky orders the woman, "Go in there and lay down on your belly." After she lies on the floor, he commands, "Put your arms behind your back."

Fearful for her life, Rosa does as she is told. Her face winces with pain as the bearded convict binds and tightens her hands behind her back with electrical wire. He restrains her further by binding her ankles together.

Wassenaar orders his partner to stand guard over the two staff members and then exits the office with a charge of adrenaline coursing throughout his body. He announces to the fifteen other inmates that have been preparing the morning meal, "This is your lucky day, guys! We're getting outta here! If anyone wants to go, let's go!"

After the other inmates refuse to get involved, Wassenaar herds them into a storage room and locks the door.

As he re-enters the kitchen's office, Wassenaar questions Martin while pressing the shank to the officer's neck, "What key opens the fucking tool room?"

After revealing which key opens the door, Martin is ordered into the room and told to strip out of his uniform. Using Martin's handcuffs, the convict restrains him by cuffing him to the pull handles of the tool room door.

Terrified, Rosa speaks out to her captors from her place on the floor, "My hands are too tight, could you please loosen them?"

Instead of compassion, the woman's plea is met with a violent reaction from Wassenaar, who walks over to the prostrate civilian and kicks her hard in the ribs. He threatens, "I am not messing around! Now you answer me! Is James coming in later, or not?"

Her reply is mixed with fear and sobs, "I don't know."

The nervous, angry convict responds with another kick to the ribs, "Shut up Bitch!"

Wassenaar's lingering concern as to the whereabouts of James earlier should have sent up a "red flag" to Rosa that something was out of the ordinary; as ordinary as things can be in an environment where one out of four people has killed someone.

Before exiting the office for a second time Wassenaar tells Coy, "All right, you keep an eye on these two while I go shave this shit off."

The "shit" that Wassenaar referred to was his annual growth of beard. The beard, this year, is a ruse to confuse a young new officer who is manning the Morey Unit Tower. Wassenaar has studied this "fish" and knows that if he looks enough like Martin, that Officer Auch should allow him access into The Tower. Auch's done it before for Officer Martin and Wassenaar hopes he'll do it just one more time.

Wassenaar dresses into Martin's standard uniform

pants, then stands at a mirror shaving off his beard with an electric razor, creating his new identity. His similarity to the kitchen officer is uncanny once he removes his beard.

Coy approaches his partner and whistles, "Dude, you really do look like Martin."

Ricky receives the compliment with disdain, "It doesn't matter what you think, as long as that kid up there thinks so."

"Think he'll pop you in?"

"No, not me, but I bet he'll pop in Officer Martin. I've seen him do it before." Ricky hopes that his years of watching and scheming are going to pay off.

He places the steel stirring paddle in the side pocket of the uniform pants and covers the handle by wearing Martin's brown ADC jacket.

As he exits the kitchen office Wassenaar warns his partner, "Look Pony, this shift is bare. They're going to call Martin any time for a 'Code 4', so be ready. Don't fuck this up."

"When do I come out?"

"When I call you and say that 'It's time to start feeding,' Pony do not leave the kitchen until you hear those words."

After the uniformed convict leaves, Rosa's worst fears of prison rape are realized when Coy approaches her as she lies face down on the floor. He violates her by stroking and rubbing her buttocks. He then walks away and addresses the restrained Officer Martin, "When are you supposed to do your next radio check?"

The seemingly in-control guard explains, "It's now, they should be calling for a 'Code 4' anytime."

Wassenaar and Coy have picked a critical hour to initiate their escape. It is widely known that on this shift there are junior officers with little experience working at a staffing level that is considered "low ebb." This is the shift that has the least staff.

So isolated and alone are many of the posts in this prison, that Central Control places a radio call to each post every hour for a "Code 4." This is law enforcement or "cop-speak" terminology for "Are you okay?" The call is placed to Martin at 0420 hours. "Morey Unit Kitchen, Code 4 check. Are you Code 4?"

Realizing the importance of Martin's response, Coy issues the order, "You better say the right thing motherfucker, or I'll stab you in your fucking head."

The intimidated guard responds by speaking into the radio held in the convict's hand, "Copy. We're Code 4."

Chapter Three
Fresh Air

After escaping from the kitchen, Wassenaar heads for the base of The Tower. He walks at a fast clip the fifty yards to the gate that allows access to The Tower area. The early morning desert darkness and air seem crisp as it always does this time of year. But on this particular morning, there is a special air quality. To Ricky Wassenaar, this morning's air keeps getting fresher and fresher as he approaches the free world air that he believes awaits him and Steven Coy.

Inside the second level of The Tower, Jason stands operating the control panel. He sees what appears to be Officer Martin standing below shadowed in halogen lighting, and opens the perimeter gate for access to the lower tower door. Wassenaar approaches the door and waits for entrance.

When Jason looks down upon what he believes to be a fellow officer, the young novice makes a decision that will affect the rest of both his and Lois Fraley's lives. The rookie realizes that he has seen this man before; it's Officer Martin from the kitchen. In the past, the young man has seen other staff members leave their posts in the kitchen to enter The Tower for a cup of coffee, a cigarette and conversation with their co-workers on the late shift.

When Lois hears the second "pop" of The Tower entrance open, she asks her coworker, "Who is it?" Jason's response is unnerving, "Oh, I don't know, it looks like Martin."

The moment that Jason responds, Lois experiences a sinking feeling in her stomach; she realizes that something is wrong.

It was later discovered that Wassenaar had been observing the operations in the lower tower since he arrived at the Morey Unit in 2000. He is keenly aware of a security breach that is totally due to complacency; the lower door's electric lock, the last stronghold that protects staff from inmates, is set on "override" which allows anyone with access to push the button to gain entry into The Tower.

Lois' gut feelings are validated as Wassenaar enters The Tower and rushes up the spiral staircase. Heading directly towards Jason, he bolts past Lois wielding the stainless-steel stirring paddle. Lois' head swims with confusion; *Who is this man, and why is he here? Is this a training exercise?*

Jason, oblivious of the danger that he is about to meet, greets the vicious convict with a friendly query, "What's up?"

With adrenaline and a hatred for law enforcement officials coursing through his veins, Wassenaar responds with three words, "You got complacent!"

The convict charges Jason swinging his steel weapon full force. Connecting directly with Jason's head, a loud crack is heard as it breaks his temple. The young man's glasses fly from his face as his tall frame crumples to The Tower floor with a thud. Blood gushes from his head wound spilling out onto the concrete while the still conscious officer watches Lois charge his attacker.

As Officer Fraley charges the disguised inmate who had just attacked her partner, Wassenaar grabs her by the hair, pulling her head, face first, hard into his knee, opening a deep gash and causing blood to pour out from above her right eye.

In her own words to investigators after her release, Lois remembers, *"Then I saw him (Wassenaar) just rear back and knock the shit out of Auch. I thought, you know, this ain't normal......this ain't acting normal."*

"Once I saw him pull that out (the stirring paddle) and hit Officer Auch, I took off after Wassenaar. I was, you know, gonna try to overpower him. And, so the only thing I had to fight with, basically, was myself. You know, fight fist-to-fist or...as....what happened was my face to his knee, needless to say, it didn't last very long. One hit, I was done, fell to the ground."

Brandishing his shank, Wassenaar menaces both officers when he spots an AR-15 assault rifle on a nearby countertop. The convict pushes the rookie's face down onto the cold, dirty concrete floor while forcefully pressing the point of the prison-made knife against the young man's jugular vein.

"You feel this?"

"Yes."

"Good, if you fucking move, this is going into your neck."

Wassenaar removes the handcuffs from Jason's belt and restrains him; he does the same with Lois. Ricky demands to know the whereabouts of the remaining weapons and forces Jason to reveal their location. In addition to the AR-15, the convict now has access to a 12 gauge shotgun, a 38mm projectile launcher and a myriad of different chemical weapons.

As the convict handles the AR-15, it is obvious that he has little experience with guns and no familiarity with this particular assault rifle. He looks to Lois and demands to know if he is loading it correctly.

The injured woman, blood dripping in front of her eyes,

squints through the darkness of The Tower as Wassenaar demands more answers.

"How do I 'jack' a round into this thing? Where's the fucking safety?"

Lois believes that her best defense is to lie and play innocent.

"I don't know.....I'm new here......I - I don't know. I'm being trained; I don't know how to do this."

This was not true. Lois realizes that telling the convict how to load ammunition into the rifle will only place her, Jason and all of her co-workers in harm's way, and she wants no part of that.

Wassenaar picks up the assault rifle and a loaded magazine of .223 ammunition. He fumbles with it while trying to load the weapon. The convict approaches Jason and crouches down to speak with the wounded young man who lies restrained.

"You know how to 'jack' a round into this thing?"

Jason considers his answer, taking into account earlier training which, in his mind, taught him to cooperate with his hostage taker. He answers, "Yeah, pull the charging handle back and let go; the safety is down by the magazine."

Wassenaar pulls back on the handle and then releases it, causing the slide to move forward inserting a round of ammunition into the rifle's chamber. He finds the safety lever and flips it to "fire."

Back in the kitchen, Coy re-enters the office and places Wassenaar's shirt over Officer Martin's head to obscure his vision. This time his purpose is not to just touch Rosa, but it is to take her sexually. In his own twisted thinking, Coy is in prison because of women, and they "owe" him.

Still wielding his shank, the tattooed convict touches

Rosa once again. This time he places her on her side, allowing him access to fondle her breasts.

The weeping woman pleads, "Please...don't."

When Coy does not respond, Rosa realizes that her worst fear is about to become her worst reality.

At approximately 0430 hours, oblivious to anything being wrong, ADC Officer Robert Cornett arrives at the Morey Unit Locker Room early for the beginning of his shift. He considers and then decides to go to his post in the kitchen to relieve Officer Martin a little early. Within this geographically isolated prison, it's amazing what a "perk" it is to be relieved early, allowing a person to be able to leave the compound forty-five minutes ahead of schedule.

But this act of kindness only places the unsuspecting Cornett in harm's way. Unaware that an escalating hostage crisis has been going on for nearly two hours, Cornett heads to the kitchen to relieve Martin.

Inside of The Tower, an agitated and highly aggressive Wassenaar points the AR-15 at Lois. "What's the number to the kitchen?"

Before she can reply, a radio transmission announces the routine movement of inmates being released to the medical and recreation departments, "Is it clear to move three 10-15s to the Kitchen and the Rec Department?"

Concerned, Wassenaar holds the radio up to Lois' face. "Negative. You say negative."

Lois does as she is told, "Negative. The yard is not clear."

Upset, Wassenaar picks up The Tower's telephone, and hurriedly dials the kitchen number in order to speak with Coy. When his partner answers, Ricky issues the warning, "It's not time to start feeding yet."

Wassenaar, still carrying the loaded assault rifle, moves towards the nearby control panel that operates The Tower's access doors. With adrenaline still coursing through him, Wassenaar's ability for cognitive thought is hampered. He futilely attempts to understand the diagram for the electrically controlled doors and gates.

He demands answers from Lois, "Which one of these opens the gate?"

At first the female officer attempts to assist him; she wants him out of there. But, she quickly realizes that by helping him, she will be releasing Wassenaar into the prison compound with a semi-automatic weapon. She lies to the trapped convict wanting to make it as hard as possible for Wassenaar to leave.

"I don't know. Like I said, I'm new here."

Once he realizes that he is getting nowhere, the trapped convict forces the severely wounded male officer down the spiral staircase to the base of The Tower. Auch, still bleeding, struggles to keep his balance as he descends the treacherous winding stairs. Wassenaar issues an ultimatum, "When that front door opens you tell me; if you don't, she's dead."

After rushing back up the stairs, Ricky tries to "pop" the Lower Tower door open. Jason shouts, "Wrong door!"

Next, the convict descends the stairs once more, dragging Lois like a rag doll behind him. Wassenaar tries the door to no avail, then rushes back up the stairs to the control panel once again.

At 0445 hours C/Os Kelley and Debaugh ignore Officer Fraley's "negative," and escort three inmates from their living unit to the Morey Unit Recreation Department and Dining Hall. As the two officers pass directly in front of The Tower, they look into the tinted lower windows to see that the lights are out; Kelley sees what he believes to be two correctional officers wrestling around or, in his perception, "horse-playing." He is unaware that it is actually two of his fellow officers restrained, bleeding, and fighting for their lives.

It should be noted that the Arizona Department of Corrections employs a large number of young people just entering the workforce. These "kids" some right out of high school, are high-spirited and still playful as young people usually are. Teasing and taunting, as well as hazing, are common in ADC, and, in the past, have caused physical injury and emotional upset. Some pranks have been so severe that they were prosecutable.

Officer Kelley tries to get Auch's attention by banging on The Tower's window. When Jason sees that rescue is only several feet away, he raises his shackled hands to show his potential savior that he needs help. Jason's hopes of rescue are soon dashed as a frustrated and confused Officer Kelley walks away towards the Dining Hall.

Upstairs, Wassenaar is still trying to understand the control panel when he hears the incessant pounding on The Tower's window. He shouts down to Jason, "Stop fucking pounding, or I'm gonna come down there and kill her!"

Jason replies, "It's not me."

The convict responds, "Stop fucking lying to me asshole!"

Officers Kelley and Debaugh continue to escort the inmates, dropping one off at the Recreation Department, then forging ahead to deliver the other at his workplace in the kitchen.

Kelley enters the Morey Unit Dining Hall at 0453 hours with Debaugh and Inmate Hudson, who is hoping for an early breakfast. When Hudson taps on the "food trap" and no food appears, the two officers approach and knock on the trap. A food trap is an open pass-through within a wall that is used to slide trays of food between the kitchen and the dining hall for what is called the "blind feeding" of inmates. By delivering meals through this opening, offenders do not see their meals as they are being dished up into segmented trays, nor can they intimidate another inmate for larger portions.

Suddenly a familiar voice is heard, it is that of the inmate kitchen worker Steven Coy. He greets the officers in a friendly manner. "Heidi, Heidi, Ho!"

Kelley, still unaware of the danger present, orders the inmate, "Hey, get Martin; I need to talk to him."

Meanwhile, in The Tower, Wassenaar still continues to struggle with the control panel as he attempts to open the doors and gates that allow access to freedom. He is becoming more anxious as his concern increases about the timing of their escape. It was planned that Coy should have been at The Tower door awaiting entry by now.

As Officer Cornette enters the kitchen through a rear entrance, it strikes him as strange that there is food out on the counters, but no inmate workers anywhere in sight.

He spots Coy, his shaved head down, standing by the "food trap." Coy is apparently talking with someone in the dining hall. Cornette turns and walks up the ramp towards the office when Coy approaches him quickly from behind, grabbing the frightened officer by the arm and pressing his shank's sharpened point against the officer's abdomen.

"Keep going."

After being directed into the office, Cornette sees Rosa bound laying face down on the floor and Martin handcuffed to the tool cage. Coy removes Cornette's handcuffs and radio, then secures him to the tool cage opposite Martin.

A few minutes later, a second call is made to the kitchen office. Coy pretending to be the captive officer, answers the telephone, "C/O Martin… Alright........I will."

Coy hangs up, walks over to Cornette and releases him from his restraints, "You, let's go."

Realizing that he needs to open the door for Kelley and Debaugh, Coy grabs Cornette by the back of his uniform jacket and heads toward the kitchen door. Handing the frightened officer the keys, he threatens him, "If you try anything, you're done."

With Coy directly behind him, a hesitant Officer Cornette turns the key to open the door slowly. On the other side of the door, Kelley and Debaugh hear the jangling of keys unlocking the kitchen door. With a powerful shove from Cornette, the door suddenly bursts open. In a flash, he escapes Coy's grasp and runs through the dining hall past the two stunned officers screaming, "Call IMS! Call IMS!" (IMS stands for an Incident Management System that alerts staff to a situation that requires an emergency response).

After nearly two hours, the IMS has finally been sounded and those officers that are among the skeleton crew at the prison quickly respond. The first phase of a hostage incident, which is the single most dangerous of any situation, typically lasts from fifteen to forty-five minutes. For this phase to go undetected in the Morey Unit for two hours in a supposedly secure facility is unheard of in the study of prison disturbances.

At first, Coy follows Cornette in hot pursuit wielding

his weapon, then quickly diverts his attention to Kelley. He pins the officer up against the wall as Kelley struggles to pull the shank out of his hands. Coy slashes his steel weapon across the officer's face, spurting blood across the dining room wall, then shoves Kelley down onto the floor. Coy resumes his pursuit of Cornette as he crosses out of the dining hall into the "blue yard."

As Coy chases Cornette into the yard, the bald inmate is confronted by responding staff. A Sergeant, realizing the intensity of this critical incident, shouts into his radio calling for more assistance, "We've got a weapon. All available staff respond to the Morey Blue Yard."

Back in the kitchen, Officer Martin realizes that Coy has left without keys. If he can lock Coy out of the office, Rosa will be safe from further attack. The kitchen officer tells the civilian worker that he needs her help.

"Rosa, close the door."

The terrified rape victim responds, "No."

As he struggles to reach the set of keys left behind, Martin explains, "He can't come back in here because he left the keys right there."

Realizing that Martin is right, Rosa struggles against the thin wire that binds her red, swollen wrists until she breaks loose. After freeing herself, Rosa slams the door closed, grabs her radio and places a call for help, "We need help in the Kitchen."

Outside in the Blue Yard, Coy is confronted by more responding staff. They order him to drop the shank, while wielding Oleoresincapsacum, also known as "Capstun" or pepper spray.

"Drop it! Drop it now! Get on the ground now!"

Coy refuses to comply, but appears to surrender as he finally lies down face-first on the ground with his arms extended, still holding the shank. When officers approach to place him in restraints, Coy leaps to his feet swinging the shank and menacing the staff. They retreat a safe distance while barking orders.

"Put down the weapon, put down the weapon! I'm gonna spray you! Put down the weapon! Let's end this now!"

Seeing that he is outnumbered and succumbing to the burn of the pepper spray, the convict once again halts, this time raising his hands in surrender to stop its further use. His mucous membranes begin to swell and his eyes are blurred with painful tears from the sting of the spray, he struggles to inhale something other than the capsicum pepper. His breath is shortened as each lung full of the potent gas burns while he attempts to get back down onto the ground, stumbling to one knee until he finally drops face first into the dirt still holding the shank.

Inside of The Tower, Lois and Jason listen to the turmoil happening outside. They hear the loud "pop" of the correctly chosen door seconds before Wassenaar, carrying the AR-15, runs down the staircase and out of The Tower to stand at its base. He is here to help Coy.

While Coy lies on his belly in the yard still being sprayed with Capstun, Wassenaar stands with the assault rifle at his hip. Without aiming, he fires a barrage of ten rounds at the responding staff. Ricky, already "in the zone," tries his best to single out and shoot at one particular staff member. He places his poor aim on the Segregation Supervisor, Sergeant McCain, who runs for cover behind the buildings while Wassenaar fires his last five rounds. Ricky later admits that it was his intention to kill his least favorite sergeant, Sergeant McCain.

The sounds of the high velocity rounds echo throughout the concrete buildings across the yards and compounds, awakening many in their prison cells with nothing but questions being whispered from cell to cell. Soon, the entire prison complex will be awake with questions shouted from inmate to inmate.

Seeing an officer in uniform shooting towards his men from outside of the base of The Tower, Lt. William Jones barks out a question demanding an answer from who he perceives to be one of his own prison staffers, "What are you shooting at?"

Wassenaar's shouted reply is followed with a maniacal laugh. "You, Asshole!"

Coy, still choking on the pepper spray, sees his last chance for escape. Struggling against the effects of the spray, he forces himself from the ground to his feet and makes a panicked dash for sanctuary within The Tower. There he will join his savior, Ricky K. Wassenaar, the man in uniform that holds in his hands their last chance for escape, fresh air and freedom; *The Assault Rifle.*

Prison Captain Michael Forbeck hears the IMS sounded and the panicked radio calls while driving around the institution on external perimeter control in a pickup truck. It seems to him to be sincere...an inmate with a gun...another with a knife.

Forbeck, not knowing what type of disturbance this is, assumes that it is an escape. He anticipates that the inmates will rush to the Administration Building to escape to the outside world. After the Captain arrives at the Morey Unit administration building, he begins issuing shotguns and rounds of .00 buckshot to staff members in hope of defending the only possible exit point from the unit.

The Captain issues the order, "If someone you don't recognize comes through the yard doors, shoot him."

He decides to issue the order to "lockdown" the entire prison, and all of its convicts. Next, he contacts the Buckeye Police Department and the Maricopa County Sheriff's Office for additional backup.

Inside of The Tower, the quickly applied handcuffs on Officer Fraley are tightening, restricting her circulation. Still in the shock of the moment and the disbelief of what has just happened, Lois' realizes that her wrists are starting to really hurt as she begins to lose feeling in her fingers and hands.

Jason, who is severely injured with head trauma, appears to be going into shock. Wassenaar, still "charged up" from the gun battle, stands near his victim relieving himself by urinating in a corner close to the barely conscious young man. When he's done, Wassenaar ascends the spiral staircase once again.

Jason's bleeding wrists also ache as he fades in and out of consciousness. The shivering young man's teeth chatter as shock begins to set in; the mother in Lois comes out naturally as she realizes that the bloody young officer is in a bad way. Knowing that he has sustained major trauma to his head, Lois tries to help her young colleague.

"Jason, are you okay? Stay awake kid, you've got to stay awake."

She tries to reassure him about his head wound with her Southern vernacular, "You're not bleeding too bad anymore, and you just got the dribbles now."

The alarm has been sounded and it is now time to initiate the Incident Management Command Center. Emergency phone calls are placed. At 0525 hours, Southern Regional Operations Director Meghan Savage is paged and advised of a serious, unspecified inmate disturbance. At 0531, Lewis Complex Duty Officer Barbara Savage (no relation) is advised of multiple hostage situations in the Kitchen, and in the Observation Tower of the Lewis-Morey Unit. At 0534, Division Director Jeff Hood is notified of the situation. At 0535, Captain Barbara Savage arrives at the "locked-down" prison to attend a briefing.

Chapter Four
Fifteen Days in Hell Begins

This morning the Arizona Department of Corrections is waking to a critical incident, a hostage standoff at the state's largest prison. At 0537 hours, the Tactical Support Unit (TSU) from the prison at Perryville is activated and placed on standby. At 0552, ADC Director Hood notifies the Lewis Compound Warden, William Gaspar, of the situation. Gaspar immediately requests hostage negotiators and tactical support from the Arizona Department of Public Safety. At 0637 Governor Janet Napolitano's Chief of Staff is notified.

Everyone is now aware that two armed gunmen are "locked and loaded," while holding two hostages in what, up until now, has been considered an impenetrable, armed fortress.

These two inmates are now holding the entire state of Arizona at bay, a stunt that will eventually cost the Grand Canyon State over 3.6 million dollars. The Maricopa County Sheriff's Office alone will send 120 employees to the prison and will bill the state for $388,000. Salaries account for the bulk of these costs, with deputies and staffers alone logging over 18,400 hours of overtime during the standoff.

Fifteen days of terror and anguish lie ahead for the hostages, their loved ones, and their co-workers, the silent heroes who work for ADC to defend the public from the killers and robbers we isolate from society. At 0718 hours TSU members arrive on-site and start planning the placement of the sniper positions, known as "hides," while a tactical plan is formulated to enter the Kitchen to free the staff hostages as well as the fifteen barricaded inmate kitchen workers.

After Captain Barbara Savage and additional executive staff gather in the Administration Building to set up an Emergency Command Center, the telephone rings. Barbara picks it up, "Hello?"

The unfamiliar voice on the other side of the telephone line sounds calm and detached from the violent situation. "Hey, I'm sorry they had to wake you. But you know, I've got hostages here, and one of them is hurt real bad."

"How bad is it?"

"It's a head wound, and he's bleeding pretty hard. He needs a doctor. I'll give him up, but I need a Lieutenant."

"I can't do that."

"Well then, you don't care about your people. Do you?"

She responds matter-of-factly, "I do, but I care about my Lieutenants as well."

Sensing that he has the upper hand, Wassenaar laughs. "Well, then give me a sergeant, how about McCain?"

The Captain replies, "You know I can't do that."

After his first negotiating failure, it's back to business at hand for the trapped felon, "You know, we are getting pretty hungry up here. I'd like a pizza delivered right to the door. In fact, make that two pizzas and a helicopter. And throw in an AM/FM radio."

As Wassenaar abruptly ends the phone call, Captain Savage hears the telephone line click down hard; and only a dial tone is heard.

After dipping into The Tower's arsenal, Wassenaar and Coy throw out two "sting ball" grenades, explosives charged with pepper gas, from The Tower's access hatch into the yard to disperse staff; all of who run for cover. The two convicts have the "high ground." During its inception, the Morey Tower was designed and built as a shooting platform to quell any possible prison violence or disturbance; not to promote one.

After calming down, somewhat, Wassenaar and Coy place Officers Fraley and Auch under the spiral stairway, down by the lower door. Jason again lapses in and out of consciousness.

While Auch fades out, Coy descends the staircase where he sees Lois and a now unconscious Jason lying on the floor. Coy throws a blanket towards Jason's crumpled body, then looks towards Lois with animal lust in his eyes. The rapist issues the ultimatum, "Bitch, we can do this the hard way or the easy way."

Lois realizes exactly what those words mean. Her heart races as her body experiences "fight or flight" with no where to run.

She responds, "No, please don't….please don't."

Coy takes control, positioning the female officer in a way that will allow him penetration. Restrained by the handcuffs behind her back and anticipating the sexual assault, Lois feels numb as she surveys her surroundings. The heavy burning sensation of the pepper spray emanates from Coy, and she is only inches away from Ricky's fresh, putrid puddle of urine and her unconscious partner Jason.

She continues to plead, "Please don't"

As the rapist clumsily continues to try to enter the woman, Lois can't help but to think of whose fault this is; Jason. Had he done his job correctly and got a good visual on who he thought was Officer Martin, maybe she wouldn't be in this mess.

Thoughts run wild through her head as she endures the rape; *Jason, why didn't you just do your fucking job and get a fucking visual? You saw the top of his head. Fuck, look up and get a voice. That's all you had to do.*

Jason awakens to witness Coy raping his partner as she tries painfully to push her attacker off of her with her legs. The young man feels helpless as he struggles against the raging pain within his own skull, wishing that there was something that he could do to help her. Lois' vaginal area burns from the sting of the pepper spray on Coy's fingers and now on his penis. Suddenly, Wassenaar's voice from the floor above ceases Coy's rape temporarily.

"Pony, is everything all right?"

Fearing that he has been caught, the bald convict is silent for a moment. Then he answers, "Yeah, everything's fine, I'll be right up."

Not wanting Ricky to know what he is doing, Coy continues his act of violence subversively, thrusting until he climaxes inside of his victim.

While sitting at home at approximately 0715 hours that morning, Correctional Officer Jeremy Casey hears a news announcement that there is an unspecified disturbance where he works at the Lewis Prison Complex. Casey places a call to the prison to see if his help is needed to quell whatever crisis is going on. After trying to contact the institution's administrative offices with no success, he dials the Morey Tower's direct phone line and is surprised to hear a familiar voice answer, "Hello?"

"Hello, this is Officer Casey."

Wassenaar's voice is pleasant, "Hey Casey, how you doin'?"

Casey is incredulous. He thinks he recognizes the voice, it sounds like Inmate Wassenaar, "Hey, is this Rooster?"

"Yeah, the Rooster's got The Tower. I'm up here with Auch and Fraley and Inmate Coy."

Confused, Casey asks, "What's going on?"

"You can't possibly imagine. The security around this camp is so fucking lax, they just let me walk right in here."

"Oh, wow."

"Yeah Casey, you talk to anybody, tell them I think there's something wrong with this rifle."

"Like what?"

Wassenaar laughs as he shares the answer before hanging up, "When you point it and shoot at people, they don't fall down."

Chapter Five
Raped and Rescued

Entering from the Morey Unit Yard, a tactical hostage rescue is made into the Kitchen by TSU. Men in black gear and helmets make a dynamic entry, shouting orders, and wielding MP-5 sub-machine guns. They overpower Rosa Garcia and Officer Martin in the office, while confronting and overpowering the inmate hostages; everyone is placed in restraints.

During a tactical rescue, blind overpowering force is used to disorient the bad guys, and to protect the good within three to five seconds. The Entry Team screams out short repetitive orders with authority, "Down! Down! Down!" The concept is to restrain all involved, until who's who can be sorted out by these highly trained "worker bees" who put their lives on the line every time that they don their gear.

For Rosa and Martin, their ordeal has been resolved tactically in, what for them is, the final phase of their incident-Resolution.

Since Rosa had received no training in hostage survival, she did not know what to expect when the Tactical Services Unit stormed through the door. The older woman is surprised and taken aback when she is treated as a suspect by being ordered to the ground and handcuffed by the Entry Team. Her astonishment becomes disbelief as one of the team members, dressed in full black tactical gear, drives his knee down hard onto her shoulder, pinning her to the ground. She screams out from the pain of the large man who forces her to press her face into the cold, dirty floor.

"Please stop, you're hurting me."

As Rosa is being restrained, she hears the welcome voice of someone who knows her, Officer Davis. He directs his fellow team member, "Take it easy on her, she's been injured."

After her release, Ms. Garcia shared her feelings with prison staff when she complained about her brusque treatment, but sang the praises of Officer Martin, who she credited with helping her through this critical incident. She explained that Martin did everything right, and if it wasn't for him remaining calm, she is not sure how things would have turned out for her.

Meanwhile in The Tower, the convicts attempt to fortify their positions while Lois continues to watch Jason fade in and out of consciousness as her handcuffs tighten even more on her already numb wrists.

Wanting Coy to be dressed in an ADC uniform like his own, Wassenaar orders Lois to remove her pants. As she removes them, her underwear also comes off, giving the soon-to-be rapist a view of her genitals. Wassenaar reaches over to penetrate Lois by inserting one of his fingers inside of her, which causes the woman to feel intense pain due to the earlier sexual assault from Coy and the pepper spray residue that also remains on Wassenaar's hands. The rapist comments, "You're wet."

Disbelief in the boastful statement and the degradation of her assaults leads Lois to angrily protest in her own defense snapping at the convict, "Look Wassenaar, I'm not wet, I just gotta pee. It burns like hell."

As more members of the TSU, or as Wassenaar refers to them, the "Dark Teams," arrive at the prison, they are quickly dispatched to their needed locations. Five sets of two-man sniper teams scurry across adjacent rooftops to gain an advantageous position, setting up their individual "hides." Tactical teams secure the inner and outer perimeters, while hostage negotiators set up a Negotiation Operations Center (NOC).

The NOC is in a drab, cramped office across the prison compound. Negotiation Team Members post photos of the four people in The Tower next to a yellow Post-it note with a handwritten message that announces their number one priority: "Peaceful Resolution." A briefcase style Rescue Phone is set up by team members who hard-wire it into the NOC's telephone system, along with a video screen that will carry a live feed of the two-story fortress.

The negotiators have been briefed that one woman has been raped already, and all are concerned about the remaining female hostage.

By 0745 hours, the five TSU sniper teams are in place waiting for the Tactical Rules of Engagement to be determined and explained for this double-hostage incident.

Inside of The Tower the two hostage takers are working diligently to fortify their position during the second phase, also known as the "Crisis Phase," of this critical incident. They remove ceiling tiles and use any other items that they can find to cover the bulletproof windows. Wassenaar and Coy continue securing their hostages in such a way that they will not pose a threat or have a possibility of escape. These two barricaded convicts have more to worry about than either of their hostages escaping or, worse yet, lashing out at them. Their biggest concern right now is being shot and killed by the Dark Teams.

At exactly 0805 hours, hostage negotiators make their first contact with Wassenaar by calling The Tower's telephone. During a short conversation, Wassenaar repeats his demand for a helicopter, although he will later deny it.

In the NOC, the hostage negotiators soon realize that Wassenaar has taken charge of the situation. They also realize that the inmates never planned to take hostages in The Tower, and it seems as though the trapped hostage takers don't know what they want. Wassenaar makes several other demands; he wants to talk to Warden Gaspar and the Governor, he wants a handcuff key and he wants an AM/FM radio. By 1115 hours Wassenaar has backed off of his request for the helicopter.

From his earliest requests it is obvious that Wassenaar's mind runs rampant with hyperactive thought. Through his frenetic demands, he appears to be rambling on about all kinds of different things; food, cigarettes, media interviews, a key to loosen the handcuffs that are cutting into the hostage's wrists.

Early into the critical incident hostage negotiators realize that this standoff could last for days. The authorities at the Command Center decide to make their first offering, an AM/FM radio that is "bugged" with an electronic listening device placed inside.

At 1120 hours, via bullhorn, negotiators play a tape-recorded message from Wassenaar's sister Rhonda asking him to end this situation peacefully. Inside of the prison, the other inmates listen to her pleas as their cell blocks now lie silent of conversation. Everyone is aware that the "shit has hit the fan."

In hostage negotiations terms, Rhonda's plea is what is known as a Third Person Intermediary or a TPI. As a rule, a TPI is seldom brought into negotiations, especially when it is a family member. The reason is that the authorities usually have no idea of the personal dynamics between the hostage taker, also known as an H/T, and the TPI. It has happened in past incidents that the person brought in was unaware that they were requested by the H/T for purposes other than "talking them down."

At this early point authorities will only play a recorded message of Rhonda asking her brother and Coy to surrender.

Wassenaar does not react well to this technique and lets it be known to the negotiators that he is angry about the situation. He does not want his personal life to be announced.

Inmate vernacular for this complaint would be "Hey, don't put my shit out onto the tier." In prison, a tier is a long walkway in front of a row of individual cells.

Tactical teams plan for the safe delivery using an Arizona State Department of Public Safety robot of the radio and other comfort items that were negotiated for. At 1725 hours, the robot drops off the items and breaks down. As if that were not enough, the "bug" placed inside of the radio does not work.

Although the listening device was inoperable, metaphorically it did put a "bug in the ass" of Ricky K. Wassenaar after he discovered it. After launching into a tirade, Ricky smashes the radio into pieces and demands a replacement from negotiators.

Negotiations between Wassenaar and hostage negotiator Jim Klein continue throughout the evening regarding the conditions for the delivery of a handcuff key to ease the suffering of the hostages. Ricky comments to Klein, "You know, this is like pulling teeth. If you're so concerned about your officers, I think that you would have sent a key by now."

Hostage negotiators working for different agencies must

follow different rules. However, there are several things that are considered basic tenets of successful negotiations, such as the rapport building technique that is known as "I'm listening" and the time delaying tactic called "blame it on the boss." But there are certain items and services that under all circumstances are considered to be "non-negotiables."

Some of the non-negotiables are considered to be "no-brainers." One would never provide weapons to people with hostages, nor would you want to provide them with illegal drugs or alcohol, since that might fuel their bad decisions. Freedom and relief from prosecution are also non-negotiable. A change of location and transportation is only allowed when it is to the advantage of the authorities and the tactical teams. But one solid non-negotiable rule covers keys and security devices; you just do not give a hostage taker, or a convict, a key, a restraining device or a locking device that may be used to further fortify their position.

At the Washington State Penitentiary in May of 1979 just such a request was made during a 12-hour hostage incident involving three convicts and nine staff members.

During this era, the Penitentiary in Walla Walla owned the reputation of being one of the most dangerous prisons in the United States. The "Walls," as the prison is still known, was in the midst of turbulent times and unrest that came from within its very power structure. The institution was being run by the convicts and for the convicts by what was then known as the RGC, or the Resident Government Council. The RGC was dominant and in charge of the 1,400 incarcerated prisoners within The Walls who walked the maximum-security breezeways that harbored open flea markets as well as lucrative prostitution and drug trades.

So influential was the RGC that Correctional Officers had to ask the Council for permission before searching within the confines of the prison, which was originally built with inmate labor in 1887.

During the 1970s, prison gang members of the "Biker's Club" were even allowed to bring their own Harley Davidsons in from the streets several times a year for a ride around the prison's five acre recreation area known as the "Big Yard."

1979 was a particularly ugly year for the prison; by year's end it will have endured two hostage incidents, a riot that destroyed an entire cell block and the longest "lockdown" in the State of Washington's history. This was the same year that Correctional Sergeant William Cross was stabbed to death by two convicts, and charges of brutality were filed against staff members provoking a walkout by prison guards.

It was also 1979 when Classification Counselor Aurelio "Speedy" Gonzalez was taken hostage for the second time. Speedy, a powerfully built man, was both respected for his open communications skills and feared because of the fact that prior to becoming a counselor he was one tough prison guard.

Gonzalez had done his time as a member of what was known at the penitentiary as the "Goon Squad," a hand-picked group of rather imposing guards who were very capable of "putting the hurt" to errant convicts. These behemoths were the first responders to quell violence whenever needed within the prison, as well as being the ones responsible for the cell extractions of combative inmates.

When Speedy was taken hostage with eight other staff members, the inmates were concerned about and focusing on him specifically with the warning, "Don't try anything Speedy; be cool."

Gonzalez's ultimatum to the inmates was issued, "You don't try anything and I won't."

After the hostage takers tied their hostages' hands with rope and duct tape, it was Speedy who suggested that the prisoners ask negotiators for handcuffs. He pointed out that the restraints would be more comfortable and more humane for the women. He also requested cushions and a bench for the hostages who were stowed away together in a small room.

In the Walla Walla Command Center, the answer was an emphatic "no." It was going to remain "no" until a negotiator, who was once a member with Gonzalez on the Goon Squad, pointed out the obvious, "If Speedy's asking for cuffs, he's got a reason." And he did have a valid reason.

After receiving the restraints, the hostages were secured to each other with five sets of handcuffs. Speedy was restrained individually, with both of his hands in front of him and then placed on the telephone to talk to prison officials. While Speedy was speaking with a negotiator on the phone, he heard a commotion amongst the hostage takers.

Shouted from across the room, the counselor heard the words that he feared the most from his captors, who were expecting a tactical entry, "Here they come! We gotta do it now!"

Knowing what was meant by "do it now;" Speedy threw the telephone that he was holding, followed by a wooden chair at the unprepared hostage takers. Retreating into the room with the other hostages, the counselor barricaded the door with the help of Carl Frank, a prison guard and fellow hostage, and the earlier requested metal bench. It was then that Speedy removed a small handcuff key from a hiding place in his belt line only to lose his race for freedom to Carl Frank, who had already removed his restraints with his own hidden key.

The prisoners were wrong by expecting a violent entry from the "Goon Squad" that never happened. Safely isolated away from their captors, the hostages listened through the heavy door to the muffled repeated requests over the next five hours from their keepers to, "Please just come out. We'll get you some coffee."

At 0100 hours, twelve hours after the incident began, the inmates surrendered to the Goon Squad. Then and only then, did Speedy Gonzalez release himself and the others.

Meanwhile in the Morey Unit Tower, after some extended negotiations, Wassenaar agrees to give up three shotgun shells in return for the "non negotiable" handcuff key with the understanding that he is to send the key back with the DPS robot. These are the only terms that are considered by the command center. When angered with negotiators for delaying the trade, he reduces the amount of ammunition to two. Wassenaar flexes his muscles and exerts his dominance early in the situation by breaking his promise while indicating that these demands were merely "baby steps."

Chapter Six
Shoot to Kill

During numerous tactical team meetings, it is validated that The Tower was designed to be, and is, virtually impenetrable to entry. Constructed of concrete and cinder blocks, The Tower is an armed fortress and stockade that stands twenty feet tall. Correctional staff feel impervious as they stand behind The Tower's two-inch Lexan bulletproof glass in the middle of the Blue and Red Yards of Lewis Prison's Protective Segregation Unit.

During a meeting in the Command Center, the Tactical Rules of Engagement or the "shoot-to-kill" orders were issued by ADC Director Dora Schriro:

1. Both inmates on roof, one hundred percent positive identification, clear shot: Green Light, Shoot to Kill.
2. One inmate with both hostages on roof, one hundred percent positive identification, clear shot: Green Light, Shoot to Kill.
3. One inmate, one hundred percent positive identification, appears with lethal force directed at hostage(s): Green Light, Shoot to Kill.
4. One inmate appears with lethal force, non-threatening: Red Light, do not shoot.
5. One inmate appears on roof with one hostage: Red Light, do not shoot.

In options #2 and #3, activation will also initiate the assault on The Tower.

An assault on The Tower may not be possible. As stated previously, this tower was designed and built with the intention that it be strong enough to never be compromised or breached by the offenders confined within its yards.

This tower is truly the house that was built of bricks by one of the Three Little Pigs of the fairy tale. Albeit these bricks are cinder blocks, they cannot be taken down with a huff and a puff and, up until now, The Tower has been considered to be impenetrable. At least that is what Wassenaar's "pigs" considered it to be, until early one Sunday morning in January, when two hard-core wolves huffed and puffed and found their way in.

Now, The Tower is being controlled by two of the inmates that it was built to confine within the Morey Unit. Administrators make a quick decision to "cut" the electrical power to The Tower to prevent Wassenaar and Coy from further control of doors, gates, and access points. The tactic of providing and disconnecting electrical power is used throughout the siege by the negotiators and the administration to barter as well as harass the hostage takers.

The Morey Unit Tower serves several purposes; while it was primarily designed as a shooting platform for emergent situations, it is also used as a point for medical staff to issue medications to inmates, a property storage area for releasing offenders, as well as an armory with several different weapons that are available for use in an emergency.

The primary firearms that are stored in this stockade are a Colt AR-15 assault rifle, a Remington 870 police-model 12 gauge shotgun and a 37 mm projectile launcher that can be used to shoot a myriad of "less-than-lethal" rounds of ammunition including tear gas. Yet, these weapons are kept unloaded, and are not very accessible.

At the Morey Unit, unlike the other five individual "Yards" at Lewis Prison, it is not permissible to have a loaded weapon in The Tower on the graveyard shift unless it is about to be used. How can this be? What if an emergency situation rears its ugly head and there is violence in the Red or the Blue yard?

How can an underpaid, inexperienced Junior Officer be expected to pick up the weapon, insert the magazine, "lock and load" a round of .223 ammunition, take the weapon off of safety, fire the preferred "warning shot" signaling all not involved to lay on the ground and not move, and then "bear down" on the target, get a good sight picture, and then take the fatal shot at the assailant who by now may have killed or maimed his opponent?

This can only be done by a seasoned staff member with years of experience in dealing with these firearms. Even then, can it be done in less than ten seconds? How many times can men bent on retaliation stab or beat another man in ten seconds?

Why are these three weapons stored unloaded? Any gun advocate will point out that an unloaded firearm is of no use. Could it be the high number of accidental misfires in the towers that have prompted the Morey Unit executive staff to keep these firearms unloaded?

The NOC is up and running with trained crisis negotiations staff from numerous different departments and jurisdictions. By the time this standoff concludes, over sixteen different law enforcement agencies will have participated, utilizing thirty different negotiators, ten of them "primaries."

The Primary Negotiator is the man or woman in the "hot seat" that is the conduit between the hostage takers and the command center. Their purpose is to keep the H/Ts talking to allow for the passage of time, which helps defuse the emotions and anger that prevent people from cognitive and rational thinking.

In the NOC someone has placed a sign next to "Peaceful Resolution," it says "Time is on our side." It was placed there by Phoenix Police Department Hostage Negotiator Robert "Bob" Ragsdale.

Detective Ragsdale is a twenty-seven-year veteran of

the Phoenix PD where he worked in nearly every capacity as an officer after serving a Tour of Duty in the United States Army. He once pounded the "Walking Beat" and later drove a radio car for the Patrol Division in this metropolitan city that now boasts a population of over 1.4 million people. Throughout his noteworthy career, Detective Ragsdale has worked in the Homicide Unit, the Tactical Training Detail, and has served as a Public Information Officer for the Department. He is currently assigned as a primary negotiator with the Special Assignments Unit (SAU), which is the Phoenix PD's full-time SWAT team, although he wasn't always a talker.

In 1985, Ragsdale joined the SAU as a tactical sniper, where he later found out that the best ammunition in critical incidents are his own words and not "168 grain matched-grade open tip," which is a common round fired by sniper teams. In his twenty years with SAU, Bob has participated as a negotiation team member in over two hundred separate incidents. His 13 ½ years of experience as a negotiator have honed his exceptional abilities to communicate with others for the purpose of resolving potentially bad situations peacefully, without violence, injury or death.

Detective Ragsdale is a trusted communicator, and is considered to be the epitome of what a hostage negotiator should be; he is wise beyond his years, patient, effective, understanding and not judgmental. This man trains and mentors others to become negotiators by instructing in a variety of Basic through Advanced Crisis Negotiations classes.

His intent this morning is to be the conduit, and to prove true the axiom that "time is on our side" by keeping Wassenaar and Coy talking in an attempt to resolve what could very quickly and easily become a double-murder. It will be Bob's exceptional people and negotiation skills along with his abilities to communicate and convince the Command Center to "bend the rules" that will be invaluable throughout the siege.

As time progresses with no end in sight, the officials and negotiators within the Command Center try to learn more about their opponents. Medical and prison records are thoroughly studied as well as electronic databases that explain a little bit more about who they (the authorities) are up against.

Ricky "Kurt" Wassenaar is a textbook case, or can be defined as a "poster boy" for antisocial disorder. Classic signs for this diagnosis started showing up when he was a young man, and culminated at the age of eighteen when he was first jailed in his native state of Michigan for attempted larceny. A year later, he was arrested again in Kent County, Michigan, for stealing a vehicle.

By the age of nineteen, he was charged with attempting to escape from the Michigan prison where he was serving his time. After his eventual release, Wassenaar traveled to the Southwest for a little "geographic escape" from the state that in his opinion was "holding him down." It should be noted that a classic sign of antisocial disorder is not accepting responsibility for one's own actions.

Perhaps it wasn't the state, but the man that was at fault. This theory was proved correct shortly after Wassenaar's relocation to Pima County in Arizona, where he was arrested and charged on felony counts of kidnapping and child molestation in 1985. A jury found him "not guilty" of those charges. So was he "not guilty," or was he just lucky because a competent attorney had represented him?

Either way his luck ran out in Tucson, Arizona, two years later when Wassenaar was found guilty and sentenced to prison for armed robbery and aggravated assault. Twelve years later, in 1997, he was paroled to Tucson under house arrest. Wassenaar was wearing an electronic ankle monitor when he committed the crime that would send him, once again, to prison for a twenty-eight year sentence.

45

The crime was the armed robbery of a strip club in Pima County, which was followed by a high-speed car chase with police and Wassenaar firing gunshots at the pursuing vehicles. During this pursuit, Ricky attempted to kill a police officer mounted on a motorcycle by running him down.

The chase ended after a car wreck occurred involving an innocent woman who had no idea that her life was about to be affected by the antics of this social misfit. Wassenaar was knocked unconscious.

Along with a propensity for crime comes an arrogant pride that often causes someone like Ricky nothing but grief. This pride was so prevalent that he foolishly undertook the task of representing himself in the Pima County Superior Court while facing the possibility of decades, or even a lifetime, in prison.

This arrogance is often present in people with antisocial disorder, along with an ability to change their appearance much like a chameleon to play to a particular audience, in this case, a jury. Wassenaar performed poorly in front of this jury by rambling on with an hour-long closing argument.

Pima County Prosecutor Rick Unklesbay commented, *"He very much wanted to control the trial. I remember him as being pretty intelligent and pretty good with the jury in the sense that he was polite. It was only outside of the jury's presence when he'd show anger when he didn't like the way things were going."*

As a wise man once said, "He that is his own lawyer has a fool for a client."

This fool got himself sentenced to spend the next twenty-eight years banished in a desert prison. At this rate, he will be incarcerated in prison until the ripe old age of sixty-one years.

Yet his poor performance and novice ability at playing lawyer did not stop him there. While serving his sentence, Wassenaar filed at least two lawsuits against ADC, once again representing himself in both situations. In 1998 he sued the state of Arizona for $25,000 in punitive damages for a "severe injury" caused while he was a member of a work crew installing razor ribbon wire at the Arizona Prison Complex-Florence. He required nine stitches, and he was determined that someone was going to pay.

His lawsuit charged that ADC, "failed to warn the plaintiff that he may come in contact with, or approximation to, razor wire." This civil complaint was "laughed out of court" by a Maricopa County Judge, along with his earlier court claim for three boxes of his property that he claimed were destroyed by correctional officers.

Perhaps it was these "perceived injustices" that caused him to go to war against the State of Arizona and the Department of Corrections. Will Jason Auch and Lois Fraley be held accountable? By God, someone is going to pay.

After many hours of negotiations, a handcuff key has finally been approved by the Command Center for delivery. The "powers-that-be" have spent endless hours discussing and wrestling with this demand.

Wassenaar has been demanding a key from the very beginning because Lois Fraley and Jason Auch's discolored wrists are cut and swollen from the restraints being too tight; they are both in pain. The negotiators have finally made a deal with their nemesis.

In return for letting him and Coy use the key to ease the officer's suffering, Wassenaar will give up some ammunition. Also included in this deal are a radio charger, some cookies, and a battery for the two-way radio in The Tower.

In The Tower, tight handcuffs are the least of Jason's problems. When Wassenaar attacked the rookie officer, smashing him in the face with the steel stirring paddle, it broke the bone in his skull that surrounds the eye called the "orbit" which will later require Orbital-Craniofacial surgery. But for now, Jason lies on the floor of The Tower in a crumpled, sweating, shock-ridden unconsciousness.

Wassenaar later expressed his dissatisfaction with negotiations during a radio interview. *"When we first took The Tower we handcuffed the officers and they did not have a handcuff key, so we spent thirty-one hours negotiating just to un-handcuff their officers. For this key, I had to give up three bullets in order to get a handcuff key to get their officers out of these cuffs, which I bolted down pretty tight. They had very little circulation in their hands, the female's wrists are still cut from the handcuffs."*

On Day Two at 0652 hours, less than twenty-four hours since his first demands, the DPS robot delivers a single handcuff key and the remaining negotiated items. Lois and Jason are relieved that Command has finally given in to the hostage taker's demands. However, the seasoned correctional officer has plans of her own in mind.

After the hostage takers receive the key to loosen her restraints, Lois begins to consider escape. Her plan and hopes are that if just one cuff is left loose enough, she may be able to dupe and kill Wassenaar and Coy by waiting for the exact moment when she can release herself to "get the drop" on her captors in their sleep. She realizes that the opportunity may be moments or days away, but she also knows that, given the chance, she will grab the shotgun and shoot both of her captors.

In return for the received items, Coy and Wassenaar are to send some negotiated items back via the robot one hour later as previously agreed. They return the handcuff key along with two shotgun shells and a 37mm. round of ammunition containing rubber ball rounds.

Chapter Seven
Death, Surrender or Rescue?

On the morning of Day Three, Lois awakens to the sounds of Wassenaar and Coy scurrying around The Tower looking through strategically placed peepholes that were left or cut into the covering of the bulletproof windows. The two reprobates are looking for and anticipating that the Dark Team will soon make their move.

Coy speaks, "Whataya think Rooster?"

"I don't like it. I think this shit is getting old, fast."

Lois hears the words "old fast" and realizes that she herself feels ten years older than she did just yesterday. Along with her sore face and jaw, her knees and hips ache from endless hours of sitting and sleeping on The Tower's concrete floor alongside an increasing amount of trash and fly carcasses. The tired woman closes her eyes once again in the hopes of shutting out the world. Her mind begins to run wild with thoughts of despair.

Lois considers suicide; she knows she can do it. Hell, inmates can do it right beneath their jailer's noses, so why can't she?

And then, for only a moment, she sees a glimmer of hope as the images of her daughter Kyla and her domestic partner Tere drift through her mind. Her heart races again, as it has for days when her "fight or flight" instincts once again kick her into overdrive. But there's something different this time, it's as if her heart is beating with warmth and love. The beautiful feeling stops as quickly as it began. Dread takes over her thoughts. Dread of being shot and killed by these two maniacs that have raped her or, worse yet, being shot and killed by TSU. She knows she's dead.

Lois' inner voice screams out, *"NO! Stop it! Lois you are dead. You know that you're dead. ADC doesn't negotiate. Get it? You've been left to hang out to dry by ADC."*

The inner voice speaks softer and gentler to Lois as tears streak down her dirty face, *"Lois think about it, you're already dead. You have to let Kyla and Tere go, it's better for them. I think you know what you have to do."*

In her own words after her release Lois shared her thoughts of despair, *"In my mind I said goodbye to everybody in my life within the first few days. I had to separate myself emotionally from my family, I was prepared to lose everything that I loved. I already considered myself dead."*

At 1322 hours on Day Three, the DPS robot delivers more "comfort items" to the hostage takers. This lot includes: one handcuff key, bottled water, two bars of soap, one pack of coffee and seven individual cigarettes.

Once again the handcuff key has been sent up to The Tower to lessen the suffering of the hostages and to allow confirmation of the conditions of Officers Fraley and Auch. In return for these items, both hostages are to be allowed to walk, one at a time, half-way up the ladder onto the Observation Deck, to show their upper torsos to tactical, medical, and negotiators for a "visual wellness check." This procedure will be repeated several times throughout the siege.

During these wellness checks, snipers train their weapons on the "T-Zones" of suspects and hostages alike.

While most people trained in firearms are taught "shoot to stop" by firing a torso shot, snipers are trained "shoot to kill." They have spent untold hours learning the method of placing a very precise shot into the T-Zone, the primary target for these marksmen, which is the T-shaped area of the brow, forehead and nose. This unheard shot ceases all movement of the Target by instantly stopping all motor function in the brain from being transmitted throughout the body. This shot is so accurate that once hit, a man or woman does not even have the ability to move their trigger finger.

As the snipers train their scopes on Officer Jason Auch, the young man appears weak as he pulls himself up onto the observation deck. He looks haggard and tormented in his blood-covered shirt with his hands cuffed in front of him; it is obvious he has been severely injured. Jason's eyes appear to be dull and listless, and his voice is weak as he states his name and badge number.

After presenting himself for less than a minute, Auch descends back down the ladder into The Tower. Shortly after, another head slowly rises through the hatch.

Officer Lois Fraley is seen and heard as she identifies herself with her powerful commanding voice, "Fraley 9119!" She has obviously sustained an injury to her right eye; unbeknownst to those examining her, it is from the man who now stands below her holding her on a "leash."

Her leash is actually a "leg iron" attached to one of her ankles with the other end gripped and controlled by the hand of her hostage taker, Ricky K. Wassenaar. A leg iron is a restraint ordinarily worn by inmates, not officers. It is much like a large set of handcuffs with a one foot chain. Its purpose today is the same as it was meant for on any other, to prevent escape.

As the days progress, it is Lois' reality that this stalemate can go on forever or it can end in a heartbeat, hers. Negotiators believe they are achieving little progress on the "hard points," which are the release of the hostages. The authorities attempt to gain control of some lethal weapons and a small cache of prescription medications by trading them for innocuous items. What are prescription drugs doing inside of The Tower anyway?

In every prison, it is necessary to dispense medications that range from the daily diabetic shots of insulin to the medications that are necessary to keep a person suffering from Hepatitis C alive. Along with HIV, Hepatitis C is one of the deadliest and most prevalent diseases that affect a large number of men who have been taken off of the streets and incarcerated in this desert prison. These medications are dispensed three times a day after the inmates are released from their housing units for what is known as "Med Call." As it happens, "Med Call" is run from within the base of The Tower.

Three times a day a medical staff member walks to the base of The Tower to gain access by presenting the tower officer proper identification. Once in, the staff person stands behind a Lexan glass window to dispense the tablets, tonics and lotions that have been prescribed to these inmates by a doctor or, in most cases, a contract physician's assistant.

While the doctor's visits are free, convicts do demand their money's worth; they expect that their prescribed medications be issued to them promptly. To receive their issue, they approach the "gator box," a secure sliding drawer that separates them from the staff, and present their ID cards to prove who they are. At that time, the medic, usually a registered nurse, checks the medications book and dispenses anything from vitamins to the necessary psychotropic meds that are so desperately needed to keep an offender at a reasonable "baseline" behavior.

The inmate then takes the medication orally, drinking from a small Dixie cup filled from the igloo cooler that is permanently stationed outside of the window. They must then open their mouths and stick out their tongues to prove to the staff member that they have not retained, or "cheeked," the meds for a later trade to another prisoner. A trade that may include money, illegal drugs, gambling debts or even sex.

Known officially as Med Call to the prisoners, it is also a social event run like clockwork. Inmates stand smoking, joking and trading stories, as well as sharing contraband with one another, while waiting in line outside of The Tower for their treatments. One of the many functions of this tower is to be a storehouse for these medications.

Wassenaar has watched this security procedure for years as he himself has waited in line for his medications. He knows that the day shift will never work for his plans of escape, security is just too tight.

In fact, it was later determined that it was his extensive time waiting in the Med Call line that allowed Wassenaar to "case" The Tower's operations and procedures. By landing a job in the Morey Unit kitchen, Wassenaar was able to observe The Tower's operations on the "graveyard" shift. He watched the complacency of the officers, and used their lack of proper security methods against them.

At 2151 hours, the Department of Public Safety's robot successfully delivers more comfort items, including food from a nearby restaurant, to the hostage takers. These items include four large cheeseburgers, two small burgers, four large orders of fries, four sodas, two packs of cigarettes and one package of coffee, but only for Wassenaar and Coy.

Only occasionally will the hostage takers share any of their food, and even then it will only be scraps. As a humane gesture, Wassenaar and Coy let Lois share their cigarettes, but only after they are smoked down close to their filters.

As the hours become days, life as Lois Fraley knows it will be turned upside down. This sturdy woman, who has always let it be known that she likes her food, will go hungry. During her ordeal, Lois will lose over thirty pounds and two pants sizes.

After the delivery, the DPS robot returns from The Tower with the bartered items. In addition to several of the aforementioned medications, though only a small part of a much larger cache, Wassenaar has agreed to release one baton round, a canister of mace, and both of the large shanks that helped the convicts to get where they are, trapped inside of The Tower surrounded by law enforcement and snipers.

Baton rounds, also known as "knee knockers," are less than lethal skip-fire munitions made of wood or rubber. Each eight-inch canister contains five rounds of solid hardwood or hard rubber measuring 1.4 inches tall and 1.4 inches in diameter. Their intent is to be aimed several feet ahead of the "bad guy," so they will bounce before hitting their target's lower extremities and abdomen. While their purpose is to knock a man down, these less than lethal rounds can still kill if used improperly, such as aiming directly at "center mass" or taking a "head shot."

Tactical Commanders and Tactical Team Leaders prepare and plan for a possible dynamic entry into The Tower. Contingency plans, as well as surrender plans, are devised by the team leaders so that they are prepared in case of anything; including tactical surrender, tactical rescue or even the possibility of "Suicide by Cop." Lois and Jason, as well as Wassenaar and Coy, listen to the sounds of gunfire coming from across the prison's compound. Snipers are practicing shooting through Lexan windows while entry teams practice breaching and entering an identical tower. It is determined that a .308 Caliber rifle will be powerful enough to be used to take any necessary shot to end this situation.

There is a plan in place to cut a six foot gap into The Tower's perimeter fence to allow TSU members quick and easy access to the base of The Tower if, and when, the order is given to begin their dynamic entry and tactical rescue.

On this, the third day of their enduring nightmare, Lois and Jason do their best to cope with the inevitable. Will it be death, surrender or rescue?

Chapter Eight
Suicide by Cop

The negotiators have decided to treat this hostage incident as if it were merely a business transaction. The primary focus of the hostage takers seems to be out-of-state transfers to prisons where they will be closer to their home states of Michigan and Maine. Both Coy and Wassenaar are tired of living in the prison in the desert.

It was shortly after noon on Day Four, a day when negotiations were not going well, that things got ugly fast. While Wassenaar is speaking to negotiators about the possibility of out-of-state transfers, Coy notices something that isn't right: scraps of cut chain link fencing material lying on the ground by The Tower. He alerts Wassenaar who sees this as evidence that someone has breached the security of The Tower's surrounding fence.

After spotting the cut fence, Wassenaar initially reacts as if he is in control of his own emotions. Then he suddenly escalates into a verbal tirade into the telephone. "Interesting. Excuse me, I've got to go right now. I think we have a security breach. They're all going to die! One more breach-everybody goes...I'm getting ready to fucking splatter brain matter everywhere if it happens again, Goddamnit!"

His face flushed with anger, Wassenaar slams down the telephone nearly breaking it. He grabs the 37 mm. projectile launcher, climbs half-way up the ladder to the top of The Tower and stands waving his weapon menacingly, challenging the snipers to act. Wassenaar knows that if Coy hears a shot other than the unique "boom" of the

57

37mm, his partner will immediately execute both hostages before any Dark Team can enter "his house" to free Lois and Jason.

The irate hostage taker points his weapon, aiming a tear gas round for the Administration Building where he has seen snipers laying in wait, and shoots. Once again, due to his own inadequacy as a gunman, he misses his target by overshooting the building.

Knowing the rules of engagement, the snipers stand down and do not shoot, keeping Ricky "on scope," all the while.

In the world of law enforcement and hostage negotiators, there is a term that is known as "Suicide by Cop," which is a cowardly way to die for a person who lacks the courage or wherewithal to commit suicide by themselves. To die, these individuals put themselves into positions where it is necessary that another kill them, this "other" usually being a police officer or tactical team member. While regular suicide victims are considered inconsiderate and selfish towards their family members, at least they do not make a man or woman who serves in the public domain take their lives for them. These cowards put the responsibility on another, along with the added guilt and angst for having killed a human being.

Wassenaar has let it been known several times that he and Coy are willing to die in a gunfight with the cops. It is his intention for some unknown reason to kill five officers, without bias as to who they are or who they work for. By firing this weapon, which looks and sounds like a small cannon, it is as if he is truly asking to be shot.

Still engaged in a tirade, Wassenaar climbs back down into the crime scene that has become his and Coy's new home. The angry convict grabs the 12 gauge shotgun and points it directly at Jason Auch's face with his finger on the trigger. The gunman screams out, "You're dying first. Are you ready to die?"

With a solid inner strength, yet resigned to his fate, the injured young man responds, "Can I ask one thing, if…. before you shoot me?"

"What?"

It's a simple request, "Shoot me in the head. Make it quick."

Surprised by the appeal, Wassenaar swings the shotgun to his right, pointing it directly into Lois' face. He asks, "Lois, Are you ready to die?"

Her response is flat, "I've been ready to die since the day you came in here."

Sensing an opportunity, young Jason asks Wassenaar for a favor, "Well, can you do something else for me instead? Can I just jump off the side?"

Ricky cannot believe the question. He begins to laugh, "You're kidding me. Brother, I can jump from there. I used to jump from that high when I was a kid. The only thing that's going to happen to you is you're going to bust your ankle, if that."

Realizing that the incident has gone south, negotiators attempt to re-establish contact by screaming over the prison's two-way radio, which can be heard in The Tower, "Are you Code 4? Are you Code 4?? Ricky answer me!!! Are you Code 4??"

Wassenaar, who has suddenly composed himself, sets down the gun and sighs. As he calms considerably, the hostage taker responds over his radio with a small laugh. "We're Code 4."

In the NOC, Jason's weary, terrorized voice is heard over the telephone expressing his distrust of the authorities. "Please tell them (TSU) not to fucking do anything else. Please, I'm only twenty-one....I don't want to die. Please, I'm begging you."

By expressing his distrust of the authorities, it appears to the negotiators as though "Stockholm Syndrome" is forming between Ricky and Jason. But, what is Stockholm Syndrome?

In this instance, it is a much needed and fascinating psychological phenomenon that may help save the lives of both Lois and Jason.

This "condition" is commonly related to Patty Hearst or "Tanya" as she was called by members of the Symbionese Liberation Army, after she was kidnapped for ransom in 1974. Less than ninety days later, Patty was caught on surveillance cameras robbing a bank with her captors while armed with a machine gun.

It was another bank robbery, though, that gave birth to the syndrome's name. On August 23rd, 1973, a lone gunman named Jan Erik Olsson, armed with a submachine gun walked into the Svregis Kreditbank in Stockholm, Sweden. After a burst from his automatic weapon destroyed the calm, peaceful atmosphere of the bank, the gunman yelled, "The party has just begun." That party was to last for over 131 hours and would permanently affect the lives of four of the sixty stunned customers and employees involved.

These four individuals would be the first recorded subjects to exhibit the unconscious autonomic response that would forever be known as "Stockholm Syndrome." This response to the trauma of becoming a victim can often be a lifesaver. It allows a bond to form between the captors and the captives, as well as vice versa, after forging a mutual distrust for the authorities.

When, and *if,* it forms, negotiators want it to happen. The down and dirty of it is that it's hard to kill someone you know.

Although, it should be noted that Stockholm is less likely to happen in a correctional setting, Wassenaar's comments and reference to Officer Auch as "Brother" are a prime example of the bond that has formed between him and Jason.

During negotiations, Wassenaar's focus and major concern is that any out-of-state transfers that may be granted will not be valid due to the duress under which they were drafted. Negotiators attempt to appease his concerns by explaining that the transfers will be valid, but only if he and Coy release the hostages.

On the phone, a negotiator tries to work the deal with Wassenaar by playing on Ricky's relationship with his sister Rhonda, "Come on Ricky. We can work this out, everyone comes out alive, and you're closer to family. Rhonda would like that, wouldn't she?"

The convict relates, "I'm sure she would. I always wanted to go to the mountains in Vermont, or the back woods somewhere. I'd love to go to Alaska. Get a little cabin out in the woods by a river somewhere and live happily ever after."

On the night of Day Four after the relaxed conversation, all involved in this lengthy siege feel optimistic from the progress that has been made. Ricky is calming down and with the passage of time he is more reasonable. As far as negotiators and command staff are concerned, this was the end of a good day.

As a new day dawns over The Tower on the morning of the 22nd day of January, this standoff heads into Day Five. Jason is asleep beside Lois, who is tossing and turning on the hard floor. She is awakened by Wassenaar, who stands above her staring down with a look of carnal desire in his tired, bloodshot eyes.

He whispers, "Psstt, hey Lois."

Lois opens her eyes. She looks across the room to see that Coy is still asleep.

"What's up?" she asks.

"Hey, I have a question for you."

Lois realizes that this can't be good. "What is it?"

Wassenaar explains his situation, "Look I'm feeling pretty tense here Lois, why don't you just give me a blow job?"

As the words cross his lips, Officer Fraley's physically exhausted body once again gears up into the "fight or flight" mode as her heart rate and blood pressure increase. Her answer is terse, "I can't."

"Come on."

"No. I can't."

Wassenaar won't accept no for an answer, "Why not?"

She tries to explain her situation by creating a cover story; a lie, "Ricky, I was molested by my dad when I was a kid...I can't, that's why I'm gay."

Her story seemed to serve its purpose, causing Wassenaar to back down from his proposition. He and Coy are both aware of Lois' sexual orientation, but hearing the reason why has triggered some sort of response. Lois still remains fearful of being approached again for sex by this predator and his partner. What lies ahead for Lois seems bleak, especially considering the fact that she shares the same living space with a convicted and recently active rapist named Steven Coy.

Steven John Coy is forty-years-old and has been sentenced to spend the rest of his natural life banished to live in a prison cell in the desert. Like Wassenaar, he is also a transplanted Arizonian who hails from Lewiston, Maine. He first caught the State's attention shortly after his arrival in 1983 at the age of eighteen when he was arrested on forgery charges in the affluent suburb of Scottsdale, Arizona.

"Pony," as his cohorts know him, has the hard appearance of a "lifer." A lifer is someone who will not leave the prison system until the coroner's office removes their cold, stiff body from inside the facility and even then, only after the corpse has been fingerprinted and positively identified. Coy's status as a lifer is enhanced by the snake tattoos that run down both of his arms from shoulder to wrist.

Coy's perverse pattern of robbery and sexual violence began sometime in 1984 when he was arrested for possession of stolen property, theft and sexual assault. Not only does the predator steal tangible items from women, but he is also known to take the safety and dignity of his victims by raping them. He was later convicted of theft charges and sentenced to a year and a half incarcerated in the prisons of the Arizona Department of Corrections.

After his release in 1986, Coy was again arrested and then prosecuted for a burglary in Maricopa County, Arizona. He was found guilty and sentenced to serve another five years in prison.

After his release in 1991, he was again jailed on two felony counts of resisting arrest and possession of marijuana, but only for a short stint this time. He plead guilty to these charges and was given the light sentence of intensive probation. However, even after being given another chance to live a lawful life, an opportunity afforded him by a gracious and accommodating judge; Coy absconded from his probation by walking away from a Drug Rehabilitation Center shortly after his arrival.

These, however, are merely the crimes that were taken into account and preceded the decision for a Judge to sentence Coy to serve the rest of his life away from society. His next series of crimes would be the straws that finally broke the judicial system's back.

On February 23rd, 1993, Coy found his way into a dental office where he asked an elderly bookkeeper to make an appointment for him to see the doctor. After brandishing a handgun, he robbed seventy-nine-year old Pauline Morales, a former nun. Later, Pauline remembered the intense fear that she felt as Coy rifled through desk drawers before forcing her into a bathroom and ordering her to lock herself inside.

"I asked him if he was going to kill me and he didn't answer. I thought it would be the end of me."

The next day, Coy robbed a Tucson shopkeeper at gunpoint while his pregnant girlfriend waited behind the wheel of the getaway car. He stole jewelry and money from the shopkeeper before defiling the woman by taking her to the back of the store where he raped her.

It was an attentive Pima County Superior Court Judge, Lina Rodriguez, who finally sentenced Coy to pay for his last two crimes by serving the rest of his natural life in prison. In 1999 she wrote a letter to the Arizona Board of Executive Clemency stating *"I strongly recommend that he not be released. Quite simply, Mr. Coy is dangerous."*

Chapter Nine
Finger for Food

By Day Five, time seems to be dragging on. A good thing for negotiators, but for the hundreds of others involved, from support staff to snipers, it seems like an eternity. Over one hundred hours have passed since Wassenaar entered The Tower and severely injured Officer Auch.

Lois has begun her daily, but unscheduled, routine of cleaning up after "the boys." Often, while one of the two is sleeping, the other holds the shotgun, keeping a vigilant eye on the female officer as she toils and cleans the cluttered, fly ridden Tower.

Another daily, but unscheduled, routine is Ricky's inspection of The Tower. Usually accompanied by a cigarette, Wassenaar walks up onto the roof of his tower to inspect *his* domain. He walks the perimeter of The Tower's Observation Deck inspecting what lies below, while cameras with extreme telephoto lenses from the press area across the highway capture the moment.

Wassenaar performs this routine several times per day with only one mission, he is looking for a power supply source for an eavesdropping device, or any other tell-tale sign that the Dark Teams have been up to their old tricks by "bugging" his Tower. Whenever the uniformed convict walks on the deck to perform this daily reconnaissance, tactical radio traffic is rampant, but subdued, over the radio earphones and the highly sensitive "throat" microphones that sense and transmit the vibrations of the voice boxes of

65

the snipers and spotters.

While one or several teams keep Target One, Wassenaar, "on scope," other teams attempt to locate a sight picture of Target Two, Coy. If they can coordinate a simultaneous shot to take out both hostage takers, that shot will initiate a tactical rescue by the TSU's Entry Team.

The "Simu Shot," also known as a "command-called shot," gives the spotter and sniper teams the ability to fire coordinated shots that will neutralize both hostage takers simultaneously; a definite component of the shooting orders of the Green Light scenarios. After establishing positive identification of both targets, the teams will coordinate their shots by counting down from the agreed upon number until the shots are fired, "Four, Three, Two, Kapow."

Although this opportunity did present itself once early in the incident on Day One, only one of the teams had sufficient fire power, a .308 caliber rifle capable of breaching the Lexan windows of The Tower.

In the NOC, Tempe Police Sergeant Chuck Schoville, who is an experienced negotiator, sits in the primary position.

Several years ago, the majority of Hostage Negotiations teams across the nation changed their titles to Crisis Negotiators. In these days of political correctness, this label seems softer, and the fact of the matter is that negotiators are highly trained in crisis situations and very qualified in dealing with hostage situations such as the Lewis Tower takeover.

More often, however, they are called in to calm people who are upset, angry or out of control to try to get them to listen to a voice of reason. The negotiator's intent and purpose is to calm the hostage taker(s) to allow them to vent their frustrations so that as time passes the H/Ts think more clearly. Negotiators can then offer help by suggesting an alternative to be agreed upon by all involved parties that will hopefully result in a peaceful resolution.

Schoville is on the telephone engaged in a conversation with Wassenaar about the out-of-state transfers that have been the focal point of the negotiations. So far, the Hostage taker's demands are:

1. That they never be incarcerated within the Arizona Department of Corrections again, ever.
2. That they are to be transferred to a Federal Holding Facility by Federal Marshals and the Bureau of Prisons.
3. That they receive interstate compact transfers placing Wassenaar and Coy in prisons closer to their home states.

Over the telephone, Negotiator Schoville is trying to sell the deal "as a good one" to Wassenaar, while Ricky looks at documents that were earlier delivered to The Tower.

"Okay Ricky, just take a good look at that paperwork that we gave you, and get back to me. That's all I'm asking. I know that you doubt this thing, but I have a letter from the Special Agent in Charge of the Phoenix FBI office. That's not the State Ricky, that's the Feds."

As the sun rises on Day Six over the Arizona State Prison Complex-Lewis, an area across the highway from the prison, which has been transformed into a crowded media staging area packed tightly with satellite trucks, technical crews and reporters buzzes with activity.

Outside of the prison, hydraulic lift platforms create temporary towers that have been placed around the perimeter and manned by armed officers who are ready to shoot. Additional staff members patrol the compound on foot to maintain the security of the institution. These officers are responsible for maintaining the outer perimeter of the incident with the intention of keeping outsiders out, while armed TSU officers are responsible for maintaining the inner perimeter with the intention of keeping the hostage takers in.

Although Ricky Wassenaar and Steven Coy hold two staff members against their will, threatening them daily with life or death, they are not the only two hostages involved. Who are the other hostages that are being held by these lone gunmen?

Along with the two correctional officers in The Tower, the Department of Corrections as well as the entire State of Arizona are being held at bay in this incident. The incident which will eventually cost the State millions of dollars, will also forever affect the lives and relationships of some of the people involved.

Sadly, dysfunction and divorce are all too common in the Law Enforcement and Correction career fields. Studies indicate that cops have the poorest records of maintaining marriages, one of the highest rates of suicide after retirement, and a dangerously high rate of alcohol abuse both during their careers and after retirement.

Almost an entire week has passed since these two undesirables attempted to escape and have become trapped, like the rats they are, inside of The Tower. It has been a long six days for Lois Fraley and Jason Auch, but as mentioned before, they are not alone.

Another 4,100 confined convicts are also being held captive in their cellblocks by these two armed desperados. That is the number of convicted felons who are currently "locked down" in their small cells or, as they refer to them, their "houses" for twenty-four hours a day. Since the beginning of the siege, the 4,100 convicts have had no access to the dining halls or kitchens, so they are fed sack lunches which the offenders refer to as "sack-of-nasties" in their cells.

Because there are no shower periods, a large number of inmates have resorted to taking "birdbaths" at their steel sinks as they are only allowed to shower once every three days when they are brought out of their cells in small groups escorted by officers.

These captive, bitter convicts have Ricky Wassenaar and Steven Coy to thank for their loss of programs for the past week. The recreation and education programs have been terminated due to an institutional need, circumventing any federal guidelines that make their tattered lives what they consider to be tolerable. Their religious and visiting privileges, through no fault of their own, have also been terminated. They are being held accountable and, in their opinion, being punished for the actions of scum that they do not even know; and to add insult to injury, it's because of two Protective Segregation Inmates.

In the other five Yards at the Arizona Prison Complex-Lewis, there is dissension among the "honorable convicts" who are angry with these two PS inmates, who are commonly referred to as the "bottom-feeders" of the prison system. These dregs of society are the antisocials that have raped and killed their victims, molested their own families and destroyed the lives of society's children.

They are known as "rats" or "snitches," and looked upon with disdain by staff, as well as other convicts who have committed what are considered "respectable crimes."

These inmates have been segregated from the general

population who, at any time, would love to retaliate against these undesirables even if they do not know them. The PSs walk with their heads hung low, knowing that they are often referred to as "cheese-eaters," "rapos" or "chimos" by the prisoners as well as the guards.

In prison there are two types of convicts; "Predators" and "Food," PS inmates are considered to be food. They live in fear for their lives even in the safety of their secure prison cells. PSs know that if things ever get ugly and a riot takes place, Protective Segregation is where the rioters will come to seek retribution by rape, torture and murder. Life in protective segregation is not good.

In Santa Fe, New Mexico, thirty-three protective segregation inmates were killed and two hundred others tortured, beaten, raped and stabbed during a bloody prison riot in 1991. In 1993 at the Lucasville Prison Complex in Ohio, four hundred fifty inmates surrendered after killing nine protective segregation inmates along with a very fine man, a correctional officer named Robert Valandingham. At this time, on Day Six of the Morey Tower Takeover, the Lucasville hostage standoff has been the longest in U.S. prison history; it lasted for eleven days.

In The Tower later on that day, at a little after 1700 hours, Chuck Schoville is on the phone with Wassenaar, who is very upset. The problem is obvious, he and Coy want "Subway" sandwiches for dinner and Schoville doesn't want to acquiesce. When the negotiator suggests cold cuts for dinner, Wassenaar is under the wrong assumption that Schoville is referring to a "sack-of-nasties."

The hungry convict does not like what he's hearing and responds heatedly, causing the negotiator to threaten a shut-down of communications.

Anger quickly turns to rage as the hostage taker screams into the telephone, "You ever threaten me with silence, mother-fucker, and I'll put you on the silent treatment. You'll start hearing screams coming out of this fucking tower!"

Without allowing the negotiator to respond, Wassenaar continues to challenge him, "Don't threaten me with some kind of bullshit like that...You want to fucking end this, mother-fucker? You want to send your fucking troops in here? Bring them mother-fuckers on. Come on, let's kill everybody!"

Jason Auch later shared his view of what might possibly have been the longest nine minutes of Lois Fraley's life: *"When Wassenaar was trying to get the negotiator to give us some food, the negotiator kept denying food so, Wassenaar ordered Coy to cut off a finger."*

The irate Wassenaar holds the handset away from his ear so that his audience in the NOC can hear as he shouts his orders to Coy. Both Lois and Jason display looks of dread and fear, they know someone is going to pay for the negotiator's mistake.

Ricky looks directly at Lois while he shouts, "Pony, we have to do what we have to do. Cut off a fucking finger!! That will show these mother-fuckers that we are not fucking around!!!"

Realizing whose finger is about to be sacrificed, Lois pulls her manacled hands tightly against her body, her eyes showing terror.

Wassenaar continues on with his tirade, "Cut her fucking finger off, right fucking now!! 'Lock and load' too!! They want some fucking screaming, I'll give them some fucking screaming!!!"

Outside of The Tower, the entry and hostage rescue teams listen to the screaming and ranting. They have been poised and ready to go at a moment's notice for the last six days. Right now they are in the "Orange Zone," which is a heightened state of alertness with a specific focal point. Their focal point is to enter The Tower the moment the "go" order is issued. They are prepared to enter quickly, neutralize their opponents and save the hostages with deafening noise, blinding light, and overpowering gunfire, if necessary.

Back inside of The Tower, Jason cannot believe what he sees as he watches Coy wield a piece of sharpened angle bracket from the Tower's ceiling. Lois begins to struggle as she enters the "Red Zone," the color definition for her current state which is commonly referred to as Fight or Flight, an automatic inborn response to attack.

Stores of adrenaline and cortisone race through Lois' veins as her extremity's capillaries constrict and her heart rate increases. The constriction of these small blood vessels in her arm will help to prevent Lois from "bleeding out" when she loses her finger. Having no opportunity for flight because she is shackled down, Lois begins to struggle with the large, bald man, not making it easy for the burly convict to callously sever her finger.

Wassenaar steps in to assist Coy so that both men are manipulating the woman into position. Pressing his knee onto her left forearm, Coy pins Lois hand flat on the floor, knuckles up. She screams out in pain as he presses the sharpened ceiling bracket against her little finger, intent on severing it.

Out of control, Wassenaar picks up the telephone and screams into it, "Mother-fucker, you want to play?? Do it Pony!! Cut off her fucking finger!! We'll show these mother-fuckers that I am not fucking around!!"

Coy applies weight to the crude knife. "You got it Rooster!"

Lois screams, "Please don't! Please! Goddamnit!" Coy presses down harder.

On a nearby rooftop, sniper teams are watching The Tower and listening to the screams of pain coming from within. Their tactical radios are abuzz with directives. "Prepare for entry. Stand by. The light is Green. Take the shot. Repeat. Green Light!"

Inside of The Tower Wassenaar hears a negotiator's raised voice calling out to him from the abandoned telephone handset, it's a woman? He walks closer to hear her voice screaming across the phone line, "Ricky, please pick up! There's been a mistake, Ricky pick up!"

Coy momentarily refrains from Lois' amputation when he sees Wassenaar lift the handset to speak, "Who is this? Okay, so what are you saying?"

Ricky listens intently, and then asks, "Who are you with? Why haven't I talked to you before?"

Wassenaar's next words bring relief to the menaced Lois, "Pony, knock the shit off, the fucking FBI is gonna feed us."

For the sniper teams, as quickly as the Green Light to kill is issued, it is rescinded by the tactical team leader who commands into his radio, "Stand down! Red Light! Do not fire! The light is red. I repeat the light is red."

Coy releases his victim's freshly bruised arm from beneath his knee. As an overwhelming wave of adrenaline

73

still courses through her system, Lois' breathing rate has increased; she is overtaken by a wave of faintness and nausea.

Jason, restrained nearby asks sincerely, "Lois, are you alright?"

Lois takes a final short gasp of air and then begins to control her breathing.

To Officer Fraley the question seems to be ironic coming from the rookie officer who allowed all of this to happen to her.

Officer Fraley's mind runs wild with disparaging thoughts focusing not on Coy or Wassenaar or even Jason, but on the department she works for.

"What the hell was that about? Christ, they just wanted sandwiches. How can ADC put me out here on 'Jump Street' like this? What the fuck is going on around here? Do they think this is some kind of game? What are you people thinking? It's my finger we're talking about here."

Then, after her inner release of rage, The Survivor Lois Fraley looks into the eyes of the battered young man who she has worried about for days. He does not look good, yet he asked about her.

Lois inhales deeply, and then after a thoughtful breath, she replies to Jason with her long southern drawl, "Yeah I'm fine."

Primary and secondary negotiators sometimes feel as though theirs is a thankless job. What was merely a misunderstanding between the Primary Negotiator and Ricky Wassenaar almost became a sentinel event for Officer Fraley.

When Schoville offered cold cuts to the hostage takers, Wassenaar thought that he was referring to sack-of-nasties. During the ensuing tirade and near amputation of Lois' pinky finger the misunderstanding was discovered and rectified by a female FBI negotiator.

Once again, after being taken from a state of readiness to within a millisecond of taking a man's life, the armed entry teams and sniper teams are ordered to stand down, and to "stand by to stand by" as they often comment about their idle hours waiting for the opportunity and the exact moment to take the "kill shot(s)" to end this thing.
Luckily, these professional marksmen are highly trained and have the ability to handle stress well. One such man, not involved in this incident is Lon Horiuchi.

Lon Tomisha Horiuchi is an FBI sniper, a West Point graduate and former infantry officer. He has been the topic of conversation in the media, the courts and congress over the last several years. Horiuchi had the unfortunate "luck" of being involved in both the Randy Weaver standoff in Idaho and the Branch Davidian crisis in Waco, Texas.
He was the sniper who killed Randy Weaver's wife, Vicki, while she held her ten-month-old daughter behind their cabin door. He later shot and wounded Randy Weaver and his friend, Kevin Harris. The Sniper was also accused of shooting into a burning building during the fifty-one days of the Waco Branch Davidian crisis. Later, Lon Horiuchi had to stand in the cross-hairs of investigations and congressional hearings just for doing his job.

Snipers are the elite of the law enforcement special teams and are picked after an exhausting process of physical, psychological and polygraph testing. In a perfect world, these trained sharpshooters are responsible for making instant life-and-death decisions under the "color of law." However, this is not a perfect world.

While the selection criterion is impressive, snipers are human. They lay in wait for hours on end, in ditches and on rooftops, in the freezing cold and the searing heat, waiting for the prudent "kill shot" that is sometimes imperative.

If a mistake is made, and a man or a woman is killed, snipers are held accountable for their actions. In this litigious society it sure doesn't seem worth it, but these men and women are the professionals that are trusted with life and death decisions everyday.

It's a thankless job.

Chapter Ten
A Long Night for Lois

On Day Six at 2041 hours, a much more rational Wassenaar decides to try another interaction with Schoville via phone. Ricky explains his willingness to cooperate with the authorities to the negotiator, "To show good faith, we're going to let one of your officers go tomorrow. But it's under conditions…if this thing drags out, we're going to want more supplies."

Schoville's voice is heard over the telephone's handset, "I'm listening,"

"We'll figure out what we want and let you know in the morning."

"Okay Ricky, I'll get with Command. Who are you going to release?"

"I'll tell you tomorrow. Just be ready."

Both hostage taker and negotiator are tired and spent after an ugly day of outbursts and negotiations. However, they both agree that progress has been made, and then they say goodnight.

Later that evening, Coy has fallen asleep by the control panel leaving his shotgun nearby unattended, while Wassenaar works diligently downstairs securing the Lower Tower doors by chaining their handles together with several waist chains.

Taking advantage of her sleeping sentry, Lois begins to fidget with her restraints in an attempt to free herself. It is her intent to just *"get on up out of here"* any way that she can so she can be reunited with her daughter Kyla. *God,*

77

how she misses that girl.

Lois has spent many hours thinking about her relationship with her only daughter Kyla, and she can't help but focus on the mistakes that she herself has made as a first-time single mother.

Lois' deepest fear isn't dying at the hands of these two gunmen. Her worst fear is her belief in the message that the Department of Corrections has always delivered, *"We will not negotiate for hostages."*

This ideology has been pounded into many staff member's minds from their very first days at the Officer's Academy: *"If you are taken hostage, you are immediately written off."*

But why? How can this be?

While not able to speak for the state of Arizona, we believe that the premise set forward is intended to prevent the taking of hostages. Two of the things that make hostage takers feel more powerful in their bargaining positions are the number and perceived importance of their hostages. By maintaining a no-negotiations policy, the State does not give in to the pressures of who and how many are being held. If taken hostage a Warden is just as "screwed" as an Officer.

While Lois works to free one hand, her chains rattle on the concrete floor. She tries to work as quietly as possible to avoid detection. Lois can't believe it, one of her hands is nearly free…she can get loose. She whispers to Jason.

"Auch, I can slip off the cuffs, I can take the shotgun and blow both of 'em away."

Apprehensive, Jason asks for clarification.

"What?"

"Auch, I can get my hand out of the cuff. Should I go for it?"

The gravity of the situation hits Jason. He does not like this idea one bit, he's already been through too much.

"No, please don't."

She reminds the young officer, "We're dead already. There's no hostages, remember? ADC doesn't negotiate for hostages Jason."

With one hand free, Lois considers her options. Jason's face shows fear when Wassenaar suddenly comes back up the stairwell, heading straight towards Lois to investigate the sounds of her rattling chains. She quickly reinserts her hand into the cuff before Wassenaar reaches her to check her restrained wrists. The convict becomes angry when he realizes that she did almost free herself, and that he was unarmed while working on the doors. Coy was asleep, and the guns were available to Lois; had she grabbed the shotgun it would have been all over for Ricky K. Wassenaar and Steven John Coy.

Wassenaar yells, waking his partner, "Pony, get up! We've got another fucking security breach."

In her own words after her release, Lois tells her story about this nearly fatal incident, *"So why not go for it? The gun was about six to eight feet away. I think I could have made it. I had no shoes on. It was real quiet; Coy was snoring -- snoring up a storm, so I know he was dead to the world. That boy can snore; I was ready to shoot him. I asked Ricky why he didn't shoot him earlier for the way that he snored."*

Chagrined at being caught sleeping, Coy grabs the shotgun as he asks in confusion, "What? Are they coming?"

"No, it's over here on Lois' restraints."

Coy can't believe Lois' actions either, this is unacceptable. "You have got to be shitting me."

"No, she's been a naughty girl. Go get me a chill pill."

The "chill pill" that Wassenaar is referring to is a tablet of Chlorpromazine, more commonly known as Thorazine. Its side effects include stupor and lethargy. Inmates who take this psychotropic medication are often walking in a manner that is referred to in prison jargon as the "Thorazine Shuffle." This effect occurs when an inmate has taken the anti-psychotic medication and appears to be "stoned" to the point that their motions are likened to a zombie or a somnambulist.

After ratcheting down her handcuffs and then administering the powerful sedative, Wassenaar has decided to place an additional sanction on the woman who very nearly got the drop on him and Steven Coy; no more cigarettes for Lois.

Ricky has already come to the conclusion that he may not be able to kill Jason if the Dark Teams storm The Tower, and that now is the perfect time for him and Coy to talk to young Jason about his fate.

Under the influence of the heavy medication, but trying hard to eavesdrop on Ricky and Jason's conversation, Lois' begins to lose focus. Her eyes glaze over, and it feels as though a "fog" is setting into her mind.

The drugged woman wills herself to stay awake; *"This is important. C'mon Girl, don't let this med mess with your mind, it's all you've got left. Don't let it knock you out....Stay awake Girl, you can do it. Kick its ass."*

She hears Wassenaar's voice distance itself as it eventually drones away to nothing. "Alright kid, it's time to talk about your future, if you still want to have one......"

Chapter Eleven
Left Behind

Day Seven for Lois Fraley was just a bad day altogether, that started off poorly and got progressively worse. Still feeling the lingering effects from her drug induced sleep, the groggy woman is awakened by the rapist Steven Coy before the sun rises.

While holding the AR-15, Coy whispers to Lois in an attempt to wake her, "Yo, Lois. Wake up, I need to talk to you."

A confused Lois asks, "What's up?"

"I've got a deal for you. It's not too bad."

She knows this can't be good. "What do you want?"

He offers her a deal, "You just 'do it' with me, and I'll help you out. Look, this is how it'll work. If you just 'give it up,' when the Dark Team storms in here, I'll give you a two or three second chance; I'll give you a two or three second head start, till I shoot you."

Shocked, Lois responds, "No. Please don't. I can't."

Coy can't believe his own ears, to him this is a good deal, "You won't do that? I'll give you two to three seconds before they storm in, a chance to run."

"No. I can't do that."

"Why not?"

Lois cannot believe the irony of his offer, "Pony, I'm on a fucking leg iron, and I'm chained to this corner, where the hell am I gonna run?"

Coy still thinks that his offer is a good one, placing Lois in control of her destiny; to refuse it makes no sense to him.

"So, what Lois, you just feel lucky?

Lucky? He's got to be kidding. Lois retreats from the moment and goes back in her thoughts to the evening when she may have said her last goodbye to her partner Tere six nights ago. She rocks and prays beneath her blanket while remembering Tere walking her to their car, as if it were any other evening. Yet, something that night felt different; not quantifiable, but different.

As Tere says good night, Lois, for indescribable reasons feels compelled to share important information that the officer hopes will never be needed, "Tere, ADC has a no negotiations policy if someone is taken hostage. If I'm ever taken hostage, there won't be any negotiations."

After listening to Lois' concern, Tere responds with a loving smile and a good word, "Don't worry Honey, you have a better chance of winning the lottery."

In The Tower, as Lois rocks and prays, she deals with her agony within by using wit and humor, *"Damnit, I shoulda bought a ticket."*

After pulling the blanket back over her head, Lois reaches into her bra to remove two hidden photographs. The woman sobs quietly while she looks at the tattered pictures of the most important people in her world; her daughter Kyla and her partner Tere.

Officer Fraley stares off through her tearful eyes into the weave of the blanket that shelters her from the Hell that is this moment. She begins to rock and think. Rock and think. Rock and think.

I'm giving up. I'm giving up you know, I'm losing faith here…..I'm not feeling very positive anymore…..I felt positive this long…….Kyla I'm sorry baby, but I don't think I can make it…..I want to die.

Lois rocks herself to sleep beneath her torn wool blanket holding the picture while the rapist Steven John Coy stands guard above her with his automatic rifle.

After Lois wakes up again Day Seven continues to get worse when Wassenaar informs her that today a hostage will be released, "Lois, Pony and I made a decision last night. We're letting Jason go home today."
   This can't be happening. Lois' mind starts to spin, she never considered that they would keep her. She wants to say it: *"What? Hey what about me? I'm the female here," but she refrains.*
   Wassenaar continues to explain his decision, "Yeah, you pretty much pissed in your own mess kit last night when you tried to escape on me."
   "Ricky, I wasn't trying to escape, the cuff was loose. What was I supposed to do?"
   Wassenaar stands resolute in his decision, "The point is, the Kid is leaving today."

The decision just seems plain wrong to the female officer that is being held hostage by these two armed convicts. What ever happened to women first? It begins to sink even deeper into Lois Fraley's reality that these are not gentlemen, these are less-than-men. Wassenaar and Coy don't accept responsibility for most of what they've done in their own lives, let alone for how they have shattered the lives of the victims and families with their criminal actions.
   Lois' mind races to the next argument she has concerning Wassenaar's decision: *I didn't get myself into this situation; I should be the one that's leaving. I'm not the one who popped the doors. Let me go. I should be leaving....I did not get myself into this.*
   But, just as suddenly as her mind reaches for blame, it redirects. The Survivor Lois Fraley emerges with thoughts of love and compassion along with faith in a Higher Power:

I accept this. Auch is a good guy, he's a young man with his whole life ahead of him. For some reason God wants me here.

Asked later about his decision to let Jason go on Day seven, and to keep Lois, Wassenaar explained, *"We released the first officer on Saturday, and it was from no negotiations. It was me and my partner sitting here and discussed that he was twenty-one-years old, he didn't need to die in here, so we kind of discussed his future with him, and he pretty much guaranteed us he was going to seek a new occupation. And that was one of the reasons why we let him go. So we exchanged him for two pizzas, six Big Macs, six fries, fourteen packs of camels and about thirty-dollars worth of commissary."*

In a letter written by Wassenaar to Arizona Republic reporter Dennis Wagner, he explained about his and Coy's conversation with Jason on the night of Day Six while Lois was drugged:

We agreed to release Jason Auch because he turned out to be a good kid in a bad situation. He was only twenty-one. He made us believe that he would never work for ADC again, and that he had been fucked in listening to the advice of his parents to take the job with ADC. The kid showed heart also. When I told him that I was going to kill him, he replied "Just shoot me in the head and do it right." That impressed me; he was just a stupid kid in a bad situation.

This merciful statement, written by the man who almost killed Officer Auch on Day One of the siege, is more solid evidence that "Stockholm Syndrome" did save the young man's life.

At approximately 1500 hours Jason dons his backpack

preparing for his long awaited return to normalcy. Coy has the AR-15 trained on Lois, who removes her wallet, handing it to the lucky young man with a request.

With emotion that makes her voice crack and her southern drawl even more pronounced, Lois asks for a favor, "Auch, take my wallet to my family. You tell 'em that I love 'em. And no matter what happens, I love 'em. And they are right here with my heart. I've got their pictures right next to my heart."

Lois tearfully hugs Jason goodbye.

After witnessing their emotional embrace, Coy yells up to Wassenaar, "Hey Rooster, you ready for him?"

"Yeah, send him up."

Jason climbs slowly up the ladder onto the Observation Deck realizing that snipers on rooftops have their weapons trained on him.

The snipers and spotters observe Officer Auch and Wassenaar from their "hides" as Jason walks across the Observation Deck with the intention of going home. He has just spent over six long days in captivity at the hands of two irrational offenders who threatened him daily with death.

The terms and method of release for Jason are well thought out plans designed with contingencies in case things take an ugly turn. *The second most dangerous phase of any hostage incident is resolution.*

The "Morey Tower Takeover," as it is being referred to by the media, will have three separate resolution phases throughout the fifteen day siege; the first is the rescue of hostages Rosa Garcia, Officer Martin and fifteen uninvolved inmates on Day One; the second is today's release of Jason on Day Seven; but the third and final resolution for the incident concerning Officer Fraley has a long way to go.

Officer Auch's surrender plan has been agreed upon between the negotiator and Wassenaar. A three-story rescue ladder will be placed up to the Observation Deck by TSU members. The Officer will climb down to freedom while Wassenaar holds the top of the ladder from above, steadying it until Jason's boots hit the ground and he is escorted away by the team.

At 1520 hours the press, as well as TSU members, are amazed and bewildered when they observe Jason shaking the hand of the miscreant who nearly took his life on Day One. Wassenaar bids farewell to the young man that he has now come to respect, asking him about his head trauma and whether or not he thinks he will be able to descend the ladder safely. Auch is willing to take the chance; he is more than fine with leaving. What's a fall from a ladder compared to a week in Hell?

With a wave, the hostage taker says goodbye, "Adios Jason! Good luck kid!"

From the bottom of the ladder, Auch is escorted by TSU members to a secure staging area where he is turned over to paramedics who in-turn place him aboard a helicopter that will fly him to Good Samaritan Hospital in Phoenix.

Wassenaar waits until the area is clear of TSU and Jason before kicking the ladder away from The Tower. Across the highway, cameras with extreme telephoto lenses whir and click as they document the release for the Evening News. Reporters stand in front of Satellite News Trucks recording "sound bites" that announce Jason's release.

Wassenaar later shared his version of that farewell in an interview, *"Auch shook my hand and thanked me before he descended on the ladder. A good kid, I hope that he keeps his word and quits ADC."*

Ricky climbs down from the Observation Deck into The Tower while Lois stands "under the gun" of Coy with his shotgun in her face. Wassenaar reports with a smile, "Home Boy is so happy, he's skipping."

Those words elicit feelings from within as the The Survivor Lois Fraley, who has been left behind, remembers, Auch *is a good guy, he's a young man with his whole life ahead of him. For some reason God wants me here. So here I sit God. What's next?*

The release and the peaceful resolution of Jason Auch is a positive sign that negotiations are working. Negotiators have finally achieved one of the "hard points" of this standoff, a hostage release; a life has been saved. It may never be known how much aftercare will be necessary to bring Jason back to the happy-go-lucky young man he used to be when he started his career in corrections only six months earlier.

Jason's father and mother were both present for their wounded son's homecoming at the Phoenix hospital. His mother later commented in an interview, *"He wanted the female to be let go, and he wanted to stay. The main thing is getting her out of there safely. My son had a fracture; other than that, he is fine. He is resting comfortably. We were really blessed."*

Officer Auch's release reaped many benefits beyond his return to his family. Within him is intelligence that is vital information for the Command Center as well as the tactical and negotiations teams. He was inside of The Tower, he knows so much; he is aware of the fortifications and the possible traps that Coy and Wassenaar may have set into place to thwart a tactical rescue. Jason is also aware of the patterns, moods and individual idiosyncrasies of the hostage takers.

The Officer is an untapped plethora of knowledge concerning Lois' future; so he is debriefed immediately after the release for the much needed information that might very well help end this thing, and save a second life.

Left inside of her own private Hell within The Tower, Lois feels more alone than she has ever felt in her entire life. She is detached and even more frightened now that Jason is gone.

Her fears are legitimate; with no witness, there is nothing to stop these two rapists from doing with her what they please. They have no more concerns of a supporting staff witness testifying about if, when, and how often Lois was raped. It's now her word against theirs; *"She said, they said."*

After climbing back onto the Observation Deck, the uniformed Wassenaar retrieves his payment for Officer Auch's release. A sniper has his crosshairs on the hostage taker who is pulling up the bundle by rope.

"Talk to me partner," the spotter commands.

"Call the shot," the sniper responds.

The spotter says quietly into the radio, "Team One is on Target One. Does anyone have Target Two?"
The different teams report in, "Nothing. Sorry, blind to that target."

"We have no contact."

"Nothing."

"Nada."

Nobody's got the shot, however they all remain "on scope" with Wassenaar, or as these teams refer to him, "Target One." There is no contact with Coy, "Target Two," causing frustration to mount for the dedicated marksmen who lie on the rooftops of the adjacent buildings for hours upon hours wanting to end this tedious siege. The convict in their sights and his partner are holding a correctional officer against her will, while her fellow lawmen hold Wassenaar's life in their very own hands; he's just a two pound trigger pull away from death.

After pulling up the bundle of food stores, Wassenaar scurries back down into The Tower.

The large order of food delivered is of great concern to Lois Fraley. She is not eating well herself and it appears as though she may be in this thing for the long haul.

The lone hostage feels dread when she hears Coy's inane comment, "Holy shit! We can do this for another two weeks." Lois realizes exactly what all of this extra food means to these predators that have already offered up one of her fingers for food earlier in the siege.

Lois climbs beneath her blanket once again in search for solace from the moment, from the reality of her situation. She rocks and prays. She rocks and prays:

Lord, please don't let them do this. Please God, don't.

While Lois deals with her adversity in many different ways, her driving force, her will to live, is focused entirely upon her daughter, Kyla. During the siege, Kyla was twelve, but Lois can remember when her seven-pound twelve-ounce bundle of life was laid upon her chest shortly after delivery.

Lois now rocks back and forth praying, while she looks into her daughter's eyes in the photo, a photo that may have prevented her suicide several times throughout the two-week ordeal. She later explained that when things were so bad that she considered taking her own life instead of giving it to the hostage takers, it was Kyla's picture that kept her hanging on instead of dropping out. Tonight, while rocking and praying, she remembers the evening of

January 17th when she may just have seen her beautiful daughter for the last time.

The evening began as all of her previous evenings had before; with Lois preparing for the ninety-minute drive that she has taken so many times in the past. Her preparation began in her bedroom as she dressed into her officer's uniform like any other night. But, this night Lois felt something different, something she remembers now while rocking and praying on her seventh day as a hostage.

As she walked past her daughter's room she stopped. She stood for a moment looking lovingly at Kyla before entering the little girl's room to place a kiss upon her forehead with her standard good night message of, "Hey kid, I love you."

Kyla's response was sincere, yet as pat as any girl her age might present it, "I love you too, Mom."

So now, one week later, Lois sits rocking beneath her blanket, praying that this was not her daughter's last goodnight kiss.

It was later revealed that during the siege, Kyla was sent off to be sequestered with family, never even knowing that her mother was being held hostage. The authorities recommended that Lois' only daughter be lied to, and that falsity was ironic; "Your mother is working overtime."

Chapter Twelve
Divide and Conquer

Who is The Survivor Lois Fraley? She is a woman who has dealt with adversity in much of her childhood, as well as in her adult life. Lois was the youngest of ten children.

At sixteen-months she lost her father to cancer, leaving her mother with the daunting task of raising the children alone on the "bad side of town" in Shreveport, Louisiana. For years Lois lived in a rented duplex that had no working facilities, no locks on the doors, and missing wooden floor boards throughout. Her urban ghetto was home to bikers, drug addicts, hookers, peeping toms and the infamous "Highland Rapist," who terrorized Bossier Parish until his arrest and prosecution for serial sex crimes.

Lois' family was devastated in the summer of 1976, when the body of her nine-year-old brother John David was found decomposing in a mass of shrubbery weeks after his disappearance. He had been molested and murdered by a friend of the family.

As a young lady, Lois' life started to improve as she became active in school sports. Her athletic abilities helped her to excel in basketball, softball and track, winning her the offer of a full scholarship to play basketball at a college in Texas.

At the age of twenty Lois gave birth to Kyla, who continues to be the bright spot in her mother's life and the shining star that may have kept Lois from committing suicide to this point.

To provide her daughter with more things than she ever

had as well as the things that every child needs, Lois went to work for the Arizona Department of Corrections, walking the "Toughest Beat in the State."

And now, here she sits, all alone.

During Officer Auch's debriefing in the hospital, crucial evidence concerning The Tower Takeover is revealed when he tells investigators that he was witness to Coy raping Officer Fraley within the base of The Tower on Day One.

After gleaning this information, negotiators realize that during earlier conversations Wassenaar has often referred to the sex offenders he had to live with in Protective Segregation as "rapos." He feels as though he is better than them.

In his statement to authorities, Auch refers to the way in which Coy was trying to be very quiet while he raped Officer Fraley. When Wassenaar almost caught him, or so it seemed, the rapist was terrified of being "caught with his pants down" by his partner.

Negotiators will use this information to formulate a new methodology for dealing with Ricky K. Wassenaar and Steven John Coy; Divide and Conquer.

Later on in the evening of Day Seven, Wassenaar talks to negotiators on the phone while Coy sleeps. Ricky has a sincere look of concern on his face as he speaks, "Okay. Yeah, well thank you for that information. Boy, I sure know how to pick 'em, don't I?"

Wassenaar hangs up the phone and walks over to Lois. He sits on the floor next to her, with an obvious look of concern.

Lois asks, "What's up? Is there something wrong with Jason?"

"No, I guess they said he's okay. But, I got some other disturbing news."

"What is it?"

Ricky shares the information that he was given "I just found out that Pony raped that Rosa woman who works in the kitchen. Lois, did he do anything to you?"

Lois looks towards Coy, to make sure that he is in fact asleep, "Do I have to answer that?"

"Yeah, you do."

"Yeah, he did."

Wassenaar's eyes narrow expressing rage at the thought of Coy raping not one, but two women during their escape attempt.

"That son-of-a-bitch. See, that's what I mean about these fucking rapos man. You can't trust them. You know, they do that kind of stuff. Me, you say 'no', it's 'no'. You know, I can't get my little wiggly thing up hard if you say 'no', it goes numb."

Wassenaar continues to simmer while Lois breaks down sobbing beneath her blanket once again. She rocks back and forth, praying until her tears begin to dry. She forces herself to continue her lament with the hopes that it will elicit sympathy from Ricky who seems bothered to hear of Coy's rapes.

How ironic it seems to Lois that by using the term "rapo" *the pot is calling the kettle black.* What gives this predator the right to speak of rapists to the same woman that he himself violated on the first day of the siege?

Left alone with these two without Officer Auch, it's hard to say which would be more frightening; the constant fear of death that Officer Fraley faces every day, or the fear that she will be raped again, by either or both of these predators.

Lois has been experiencing feelings of abandon and isolation since Jason was released. Over the following days her pessimistic feelings of loneliness and dread begin to overtake what was once an optimistic woman.

But, it will be the small things in Lois' life as a hostage that help her to hang on to her own reality; the pictures that she has of her daughter and partner, and the small AM/FM radio that reports the words of prayers and support from the community, the state, and the nation. These three flickering candles of love evolve into guiding lights during her bleakest moments of darkness and despair. They are beacons of hope for The Survivor Lois Fraley.

As stated earlier, Wassenaar's favorite sister, Rhonda Krenz, was contacted by ADC officials and advised of her brother's situation and status at the beginning of the Morey Tower Takeover. An earnest plea was made by administrators asking for her help in saving the lives of four people, with emphasis being placed on her little brother, Ricky.

Rhonda hesitated about and resisted getting involved with the authorities concerning the siege at first. In the past her family has had some bad dealings with law enforcement.

After some consideration, Rhonda finally gave in and allowed negotiation team members to record her voice over the telephone with the intention of making a plea to her brother Ricky, to end this thing; to save his own life.

The negotiators make the hostage takers' survival the focus of their request to Wassenaar and Coy's families for help. The decision to reach out to these significant others was a difficult one to make, as one of the basic tenets of successful negotiations is to refrain from involving relatives due to the possibility that an unknown family dynamic may rear its ugly head.

Therefore, deciding to allow Ricky's Sister Rhonda and Coy's Uncle Bob to act as Third Party Intermediaries (TPIs) was discussed at length, while the relationship between these relatives and siblings was examined very closely. The decision to go with a TPI was made with much trepidation, along with specific rules and guidelines to cover the State's "ass" in case things get ugly.

The FBI foots the bill to bring Coy and Wassenaar's families all the way across country, feeding and lodging them in a cheap Buckeye motel. For Wassenaar's family the idea of a free vacation in the "Valley of the Sun" sounds pretty good.

It should be noted that the majority of corrections and law enforcement hostage negotiators throughout our nation are trained in the basic, as well as advanced methodology of negotiations by FBI instructors. This can strike some as odd when you consider the past failures of their own Negotiators and Hostage Rescue Teams; Ruby Ridge, the Branch Davidians in Waco and several other negotiation nightmares.

But, it is the unheard of successes that heavily outweigh the FBIs highly publicized errors. It was after eighty-one days of negotiations that the FBI scored a decisive victory in the Justus Township in Montana by facilitating a peaceful surrender of the anti-government activists known as the Freemen.

The truth of the matter is that hostage negotiation is not an exact science of the mind, and negotiators do learn from their mistakes as well as the mistakes that are made by others. It's very easy to be an "armchair quarterback" long after the stress and the tension of protracted standoffs dissipate.

But, one must consider that until 1971 in Attica, New York, and 1972 at the Munich Olympic grounds, negotiation was not used very often as a tactic to bring about a peaceful resolution. The point being that the history of modern hostage negotiations is really only a little over thirty-years-old. Taking that into account, negotiators have learned quite a lot in this relatively short amount of time.

Out of the imperfect science of the mind that we call hostage negotiations, has evolved a new methodology that is known as Hostage Survival.

After analyzing what has gone wrong and what has gone right during thousands of critical incidents throughout the years, positive as well as negative patterns are found that remain consistent. Certain rules and guidelines for hostage survival have evolved from these years of research that prove a hostage can greatly decrease their chances of injury or death while increasing their chances of survival. By acting in a specific manner, hostages can increase their odds of coming out of a critical incident alive.

These techniques and guidelines are taught to correctional staff in many states, unfortunately, Arizona pales in comparison when it comes to their training.

As the sun rises over the Arizona desert, this siege moves into Day Nine, rapidly approaching several other noteworthy US prison hostage situations in duration.

In Huntsville, Texas in 1974, three hostage takers held seventy inmates and eleven citizens hostage for ten days when they stormed and took control of the Prison's Education and Library facilities. One hostage taker was apprehended and two killed when all three attempted to escape during the standoff. Unfortunately, the death toll was four; a hostage was also killed.

Today the Morey Tower Takeover is also rapidly approaching the US prison hostage record of eleven days which was set in the Spring of 1993 at the penitentiary in Lucasville, Ohio. In this earlier mentioned Easter incident, of the twelve guards that were taken hostage, one of them, Officer Valandingham, was killed along with nine Protective Segregation inmates.

This lengthy record slightly overshadows the Federal Penitentiary in Atlanta, Georgia, where Cuban detainees held more than 100 hostages for eleven days in 1987. The good news is that this situation was resolved peacefully after a negotiated settlement with no deaths.

In a baseball analogy, negotiators involved with these incidents are batting .333, qualifying them for the Hall of Fame. But in life or death situations, this statistic is not acceptable.

The long hours of the Morey Tower Takeover have lasted for days, dragging into a second week for the captors and their lone hostage. As the week progresses, the days are blurring in Lois' mind as her boredom grows. Coy and Wassenaar waste their time playing card games and telling stories, while The Survivor Lois Fraley prays and dreams of someday holding her daughter Kyla again. She knows that in her life she has taken things for granted; she vows to change if only God will let her.

If God will let her walk out of this tower, she will be a changed woman, and never take life and laughter for granted again.

After her release Lois shared her sentiment, "I had been ready to die from the day they came in. Oh, I still get chill bumps. I took my family for granted, and I won't ever do that again."

Whenever Wassenaar is up walking on the Observation Deck, Lois is seated on the floor with Coy pointing the AR-15 directly in her face. Regardless of the fact that one wrong word might cause the trigger to be pulled, she uses her time alone with Coy to talk to him and to "get into his head" about his life and personal things such as family, future, or the possible lack thereof.

These lengthy conversations were almost always held while Lois was "under the gun." Officer Fraley knows the rules of engagement established by these two desperate convicts; *if a shot is heard from above, Green Light, kill Lois.*

The spotters and snipers are locked onto Target One while Wassenaar strolls along the Observation Deck still dressed in Martin's ADC uniform. When he climbs partway up a pole to adjust a video camera's angle above The Tower, sniper teams hope for a visual and a "lock" on Target Two. If they can get both of the hostage takers "on-scope" then they can end this situation with a "Simu Shot."

As the days continue to drag on, The Tower has become a place of monotonous routine. Wassenaar spends most of his time creating new recipes from the cache of food that he has bartered for, while Coy watches and waits for his issue of their edible profits, neither one sharing much of this bounty with Lois. Most days Lois is fortunate to eat one meal consisting mostly of the hostage taker's unwanted scraps.

The majority of Lois' time, when not cleaning or watching Coy and Wassenaar gorge themselves with food, is spent listening to the two rapists speak of their past exploits; most of them tragic and devastating to others.

When Lois separates herself from the hostage takers' conversations, she listens to her "lifeline," the AM/FM radio that broadcasts throughout the day, updating hourly her situation for the listeners in the greater metropolitan Phoenix area.

As she listens to the radio broadcasts of news reports, it reinforces the disparity of her situation, but The Survivor Lois Fraley also hears something much more powerful; the prayers and the hopeful wishes from across the state and the entire country. She listens to a report of a fund-raising motorcycle ride given in her name, along with the daily stories of prayer vigils, and yellow ribbons being worn by other officers throughout the nation.

Later in her own words, Lois would pay homage to the device that helped her to hang on throughout the siege, *"That radio was my lifeline."*

Locked inside of The Tower, far away from the rest of the world, Lois ponders her aloneness and abandonment, not knowing whether today will be her last.

While the radio broadcasts bring hope to Lois, despair is also prevalent due to the uncertainty of her situation. Lois feels positive one moment, only to have her emotions plummet in the next as she realizes that any glimmers of hope seem to be heavily outweighed by the realities of the moment; she fears an attack from TSU.

Lois assumes that the special paramilitary teams are staged outside. She knows that the snipers are prepared to shoot and the entry teams are ready to respond with a dynamic entry in a split-second's notice.

Feelings of dread and uncertainty weigh heavily on Lois as she wonders: *God, when are they going to storm The Tower?*

Chapter Thirteen
The Teams

Day Nine was another crucial day for the tactical teams as they attempt to use the negotiators for tactical support with the intention of "setting up" Wassenaar and Coy for a dynamic entry and hostage rescue. Having already set a pattern with earlier checks, the plan is to try to have Lois placed up on the Observation Deck by herself for another health and welfare check, only this time The Teams want her on top of the deck.

If they get Lois on the deck with a hostage taker, snipers will "take him out" with a well placed shot, and then an Entry Team will rescue Officer Fraley while another team breaches The Tower to neutralize Coy.

It's more likely that neither Wassenaar nor Coy will show themselves at all. In that case, if they do put Lois on the Observation Deck alone, a "fire team" will place gunfire on the access hatch of The Tower to keep the hostage takers inside.

At the same time, an entry team will blow out the side of The Tower with explosives while another team removes Lois from the Observation Deck, leaving Coy and Wassenaar resigned to their fates.

Officer Fraley once again feels alone. She feels as though, in prison verbiage, she has been "Put out on front street" by ADC. And now, they want her to do what? She is supposed to go up on a different part of the Observation Deck with no good reason why.

As Lois rises through the access hatch slowly she can

see a sniper team lying on a rooftop parallel to her position, and she knows that there are many more "Dark Teams" out there drawing beads upon her with their weapons. Lois lost her faith in the authorities when the negotiator named Schoville almost cost her a finger because of his own stubbornness.

Outside of The Tower, TSU members "stack up" prepared for what may be a life saving entry. On other rooftops, this is the moment of truth for the sniper teams. The individual sniper may be a part of the Big Brown Machine, as the ADC is called, but right now his entire focus is upon The Tower's hatch. The Teams prepare for the split-second when everything and everyone that is to be involved in this tactical rescue takes action. The sniper's shot will not only kill a man, but it will also be the "command" signal that will set forth a first-wave of fury and explosive charges that may, or may not, save Officer Fraley's life, as well as take the lives of the two hostage takers who have decided to "play for keeps."

The Tactical Teams are a necessary element in any correctional system or law enforcement community that is made up of a dedicated group of individuals. As there are very few female team members, "the teams" are essentially a Men's Club and, at times, can even be considered a Boy's Club due to the sophomoric attitudes, the flow of testosterone and the bravado of those who volunteer for the positions.

These positions include: Spotters, Snipers, Riot Squads, Entry Teams, Arrest Teams, Shotgun Teams, Negotiators, Medics and even Chaplains.

Each individual team member adds an interesting human dynamic to this slightly eclectic group that come together to form a cohesive unit, necessary for the abatement of critical incidents and the survival of each other.

These emergencies can include: riots, hostage takings, gang violence and civil disobedience. The Teams are used as support during executions to prevent the anti-death penalty protesters from attacking their conservative opponents, who believe in the biblical proverb, "an eye for an eye."

These "men's men" train together, and when they train, they train hard. They experience and endure certain rites of passage such as gas, guns, grenades and physical force. They suit up in the "Red Man" gear that is supposed to protect team members from the batons and the knuckles of their teammates who try to take them down into restraints. They "eat the gas," whether it is OS, CS or the newest pain compliant spray: Oleoresincapsacum also called "Capstun."

Team Members temporarily blind and deafen themselves and each other with diversionary devices called "flash bang" grenades. They shock each other with a variety of electronic immobilization devices, and they practice counter joint techniques and hair holds, as well as carotid submission holds, or "chokeholds," to learn how to render their opponents unconscious. They waylay each other with shields, and beat upon each other with wooden batons and metal "asps."

But, the end result is that they are a "Team." A group that unconditionally trusts each other as well as their team leaders so that they can wage war against those who initiate it.

The dictum of the Teams is "If you want peace, you prepare for war."

After being prepared for entry, the Teams are once again

taken from a state of readiness to an order to "stand down and stand by." Officer Fraley is not allowed on top of the deck, but is only allowed to show herself through The Tower's access hatch while Wassenaar holds her "leash."

Day Ten in The Tower and in the NOC was a day without much adversity or victory. Minor barters of comfort items included clean blankets and towels that were traded for another visual wellness check of Lois, with the hopes of a tactical rescue. However, the two cornered convicts were once again too wise to place Lois up on the Observation Deck alone.

Time seems to drag on for all involved.

During the evening of Day Eleven, after a series of negotiations, Wassenaar waits to speak with his sister Rhonda over the telephone. The phone rings and Ricky answers to hear Rhonda's voice.

"Ricky? Is that you?" an unsteady voice asks

Wassenaar's voice emotes pleasure in hearing his sister's voice, "How you doing sweetie pie? What are you doing out here in Arizona?"

"I *should* be lying by the pool. Little brother, what are you doing up there?"

"Just making a statement darlin'. Me and my partner just kind of got ourselves all jammed up"

"When you do things, you do them big, don't you?"

"You know me."

"Yeah, I do. That's why they asked me to come all the way out here to talk to you."

Ricky inquires, "On whose dime?"

"The Federal Bureau of fucking Investigations, that's whose dime."

"Are you taking advantage of that?"

"Oh hell yeah. Me and Renae and Ronnie are not going to miss out on a chance to spend some Federal dollars. You know that. I didn't have any idea how much Ronnie can eat when he doesn't have to pay for it."

"I hear ya. Me and Pony, that's my partner, are up here eating like big dogs too. How is my bro doing anyways?"

"Well, you know. He's Ronnie, he hasn't changed much."

Wassenaar asks,"Neither have we, right?"

"Are you shittin' me little brother? You should see these lines on my face. The years have not been kind."

"Oh, I doubt that. You've always been a babe."

Rhonda asks the big question," So Ricky, what's up?"

"Well, I got myself into a little jam, that's all."

"No shit."

"Yeah, but the truth of the matter is, I'm gonna come out of this one of two ways, alive or dead, and to be honest with you, I'm okay either way."

Rhonda's voice projects sadness at the thought, "Well, I'm not"

"I'm fine"

"Well, I'm not. Ricky I love you. You really need to consider coming down from there. You've made your point. You've won. You've left your mark."

Ricky continues," Well, I've still got more to say."

"Like what?"

"This ADC blows, Rhonda. They don't give a shit about their own people. Take Lois, it's like they don't even care about her."

Rhonda attempts to reason with her misguided little brother. "But they do. I care about her. Ricky, she has the sweetest little girl."

Ricky's response is matter-of-fact, "Hell, I care about Lois too. I said I'd exchange her for a male…If they were so damned concerned about her, they would do that."

"They're in a bad spot baby, and you put them there. You have kicked their asses. Man, you have brought National attention to this place out here."

"Really? It's not just a local thing?"

His sister explains, "No, it's National, that's why they have to stand behind this transfer thing that they're promising you."

Wassenaar debates the fact, "Now, I know about that. I know the law. That transfer isn't worth the paper it's printed on."

"Ricky, I've talked to the FBI, that Dora woman even signed it off. She's in charge of the ADC or something."

"I'm telling you Big Sister, it don't matter. They're under duress. It's like that deal with the devil thing."

Rhonda continues to sell the idea, "I'm telling you, this fucker is on the fucking up and up. I swear to God, Ricky with all my heart I believe these fuckers."

"It's not worth didley, honey."

"With everything I am, with everything I got, you know, I'm not just some gullible naïve little…They want to make this work."

"Hey Rhonda, we've been up here for over ten days now. I'm fine. I just have to decide if I want to go out in a blaze of glory, or die in this fucking prison system."

"Ricky, I love you to death. Wild horses couldn't drag me outta here…I need you, Ricky. I'm not ready to say goodbye to you."

Wassenaar reminisces, "I'm not either. But hey, you remember that train trestle we grew up with at Plaster Creek?"

"Yeah."

"If things don't work out our way, uh, that's where I want you to spread my ashes."

Rhonda pleads, "Baby, I'm not ready to say goodbye to you. I'd rather have you in a prison where I can come see you than spread your ashes. I love you, I need you," she sobs.

"Shut up girl. I'm fine. I just hate this fucking desert. I miss the seasons"

"Then, get out of Arizona. Come home Ricky."

"I wish it was that easy."

Rhonda offers her brother an option. "I can't take it Ricky, there's a light at the end of this tunnel, man…check it out. If you don't like it, then string yourself up with some socks or something."

"Always the optimist, aren't you Babe? You remember that Cagney movie 'White Heat'? When the cops corner that guy way up on the gas tower?"

"Yeah."

"You remember him saying, 'Look at me now Mom, I'm on top of the world'? He climbs up there and all the police are chasing him, and the thing blew up. He went out with a bang. That's not such a bad way to go."

"I don't want you to go."

"If it happens, it happens."

In the NOC, negotiators listen as Wassenaar ends the call. Ricky's cavalier attitude towards death is a bad thing for the administration. To successfully negotiate any hostage situation, there are three elements that must be present: Time, Containment, and a willingness to live on the part of the hostage taker(s). This is why it is almost impossible for trained negotiators to deal with religious zealots, such as the 9/11 terrorists. Their quest for martyrdom would have made it impossible to get them to listen, and to think reasonably.

The fact that Wassenaar has stated several times that he

doesn't care if he or Coy live or die is very troubling to the negotiations team and the Command Center.

Since entering the tower, Wassenaar and Coy continue to discuss their agreed upon "death wish" should they fail. The Survivor Lois Fraley prays that they don't. *Please God, let's end this thing, I miss my family, I want to go home.*

As the days of despair seem to be never-ending, Lois Fraley's life in The Tower fills with depression. Wassenaar and Coy have expressed a myriad of different emotions, making it even harder for Lois to figure out their individual "stands" concerning the siege. At any time one of her captors can assume the roll of "the bad guy" while the other plays the "good."

Even though the out-of-state transfers are the primary focus for the hostage takers, Ricky still seems to be hellbent on violence as he continues to speak to Lois and Coy of gunfights with the cops. "Yeah, bring those motherfuckers on. Come on SWAT, bring your asses out"

At those words, Lois feels her heavily depleted stores of adrenaline course once again through her veins, leaving her stomach empty with a feeling of nothingness.

Lois replies, "Ricky, please. Let's just end this thing, I want to go home."

Wassenaar responds with disregard, "It don't matter Lois, Pony and I came in here willing to die. We've got no problem taking out some "pigs" on our way out either."

Lois interrupts, "Look, why don't you guys just let me go then? I want no part of this, I'm not a violent person."

Wassenaar responds with disdain and hatred for all law enforcement, "Yeah, but Lois you're a part of the system."

Chapter Fourteen
The Suits

The Command Center is the nucleus of this critical incident. It is where the executive staff, "the suits," are working to end a possibly fatal situation. Today, this standoff has moved into Day Twelve, surpassing any other prison hostage takings in the history of the United States.

The Command Center, or simply "Command" as it is known in emergency response situations, is the place where the administrators facilitate communications, problem solving, decision making and control of the incident. While there are many different responsibilities within the Command Center, which essentially is a "Think Tank," from the highest level of decision making to the basics of support services, they are all essential.

The command structure includes: Incident Commanders, Tactical Commanders, Negotiation Team Leaders, Perimeter Commanders, Intelligence Officers and Public Relations Officers. These are just several of the approximately twenty positions that are held accountable for this incident. Each is a necessary component in charge of making this emergency situation run as smoothly as possible.

In the Command Center at the Arizona Prison Complex-Lewis, the timekeeper is a necessary entity for ensuring that everyone who is working receives payment, and this is no small order. In this situation, over 1.6 million dollars of overtime will be paid to ADC employees alone, who racked up 18,444 total billable overtime hours. An additional $535,000 will be spent on other corrections staff members who have been brought into town, fed and boarded.

In most Command Centers, and specifically within the Arizona Department of Corrections, you will find a primarily male dominant working society. Though the majority of executive positions are held by men, the true "keeper-of-all" in this desert prison is ADC's newest Director, Dora Schriro.

Ms. Schriro grew up the oldest of her three siblings in a family where her father was an aerodynamic engineer and her mother a teacher. But, it was her grandfather Michael whose influence opened her mind to her future career in the corrections system.

After graduating from high school, Dora received a bachelor's degree in sociology, a master's degree in psychology, an education degree and a law degree all from different colleges including Columbia University in the city of New York.

Ms. Schriro began her career in corrections in the early 1970s, and it was her three decades of experience which prepared her to take the job as ADC Director in late 2003. Dora inherited a prison system that was considered by many to be a "mess," that was leftover from previous administrations. While many of the "good old boys" in ADC were skeptical about the Director's position being filled by a woman, Dora was given the opportunity to prove her worth hardly six months after taking the job, the opportunity to effectively handle a hostage situation in one of her prisons.

From Day One, while the media was putting constant pressure on her to storm The Tower and take out the inmates, Dora refused to put the hostages' lives at risk and proceeded to call in thirty different negotiators from various agencies to try to defuse this delicate situation.

While any of the previous directors might have stormed The Tower with the "no negotiations" mentality of ADC, Dora refused to resort to that option; later ending this situation through skilled negotiators.

It is this woman's cool head that prevails in the Command Center while working directly with Governor Janet Napolitano to end this siege peacefully.

In a statement after the siege, Lois shared her feelings about her boss, *"I am alive today because Dora had patience. If Terry Stewart had still been director of DOC, I'd be dead now because he would have stormed The Tower, and they'd have killed me."*

Dora's response to the comment was shared with a tear, "You don't expect that kind of recognition. Pretty cool."

Dora Schriro isn't the only female in power during this time of crisis. Behind her, backing all of her decisions to help resolve this brutal situation, is the Governor of Arizona, Janet Napolitano.

Janet was born in New York City and raised in Albuquerque, New Mexico. She moved to Arizona in 1983 to practice law, and was later appointed United States Attorney for the District of Arizona by President Bill Clinton in 1993. In 1998 she ran for and was elected to the position of State Attorney General. It was only one year earlier that Ms. Napolitano took office as Governor after winning the 2002 election with forty-six percent of the vote.

Along with the office, this talented executive inherited the state of Arizona's one-billion dollar deficit. Without raising taxes or cutting funding for education, the new Governor not only eliminated the deficit, but completely reformed Arizona's Child Protective Services by designating new funding for the abused and neglected children of the State.

Governor Napolitano had also been instrumental in early childhood education by creating voluntary kindergarten programs to prepare children for elementary school. While holding office, her focus has been on preparing students for life outside of school to help secure and stabilize growth in the high-tech industries of Arizona.

Though education is her primary focus, Governor Napolitano is also very intent on the security of Arizona; law-enforcement and border control. Her efforts are responsible for the creation of the Arizona Counter-Terrorism Information Center, an agency that is focused on 24/7 intelligence to keep Arizona's cities and borders safe.

But, now her primary focus and all of her attention is on this prison in the desert where one of *her* employees is being held hostage by two of her inmates.

The remote location of this facility in the middle of nowhere, and close to nothing, has caused this incident to generate a large amount of hotel and food costs which will result in a windfall benefiting the small community of Buckeye, Arizona, with a "townie" population of 6,500. The Buckeye Fire Department will earn $55,000 for their stand by status alone. Add to the mix, the other 4,100 prisoners who are "locked down" in their prison cells for weeks on end, incurring additional expenses for food and beverages. Some ancillary expenses will include $850,000 paid to over a dozen outside agencies for support. The Maricopa County Sheriff's office will charge the State of Arizona $388,000. The Department of Public Safety will be paid $279,000 for everything from staff overtime, to the use of their helicopter and robot. The Tucson Police Department will charge $14,000 to house and feed their officers and support staff that came to assist ADC.

The total bill for this standoff comes to over 3.6 million dollars, which in Arizona is enough money to incarcerate one hundred-eighty inmates for an entire year.

Prison spokeswoman Cam Hunter commented about the cost, "It took what it took. *It took a large scale effort in terms of personnel for tactical, negotiation, intelligence and command expertise.*"

On Day Twelve, the Command Center has made the long awaited decision to allow the hostage takers to have an over-the-telephone interview that will be played on a Phoenix news radio station. To the Primary Negotiator, this is the best decision that Command has made in the last twelve days, as this simple demand has been promoted positively by the Hostage Negotiations Team to the Command Center from the beginning of the siege. It should be noted that at times the Command Center can seem to be a "thorn in the side" of the negotiators who are trying to be the spokespeople as well as the conduit of the hostage taker's demands.

Earlier the technique of "blame it on the boss" was discussed as a stalling technique used by trained negotiators to buy time during the negotiations. It actually works well, because at times the frustrations expressed to the hostage takers are not an act, but heart felt emotions. It can be frustrating to a Primary Negotiator, and the rest of the negotiation team, to make forward progress in an incident, only to be held back and tied down by the bureaucracy that is known as "Command."

As a part of the negotiations process for the radio interview, Wassenaar agrees to allow Lois to speak by telephone with a medical staff member and answer questions concerning her health.

After the deal was offered, Wassenaar approached Lois with the news, "Lois, we've made a deal for a telephone physician's check with you. Let me ask you this. Do you want to go home today?"

Lois doesn't need to think too long before answering, "Of course I do. Are you going to let me on up out of here Ricky?"

"Only on one condition, I need them to send me another officer, and it has to be a male."

Officer Fraley's hopes are quickly dashed, "Damn it, that's not going to happen and you know it."

"Yeah, you and me may know it, but I've got a plan. If you want to leave here alive, you'd better play along. Got it?"

"What do you want me to do?"

"Lois, you've got to lie to the doctor and convince him that you need to be released so that you can get medical."

"How?"

"I don't give a shit. Make something up."

Lois does not like being put in this position; sure she'd like to go home, but she doesn't want Wassenaar and Coy to replace her with a male officer, as she is certain that his life span would be shortened considerably.

Holding the phone while Wassenaar hovers nearby listening, Lois is at first apprehensive about speaking with the doctor on the other end of the line. As is natural for a long term hostage, her confidence in the authorities has been going downhill with the passage of time.

Lois answers questions about her health hesitantly until suddenly she breaks into a broad smile; something has finally gone right. The medic has just asked her a specific question concerning a recent bout with bronchitis. Only Lois' family could possibly know about her recent illness; Officer Fraley realizes that her loved ones are near.

In an interview after Lois' release, she shared her feelings at that moment:
"The doctors had asked me some questions when they were doing a medical evaluation, and they asked me about my bronchitis, and that's when I knew that my family members were there at the prison, because nobody else knew I had bronchitis. I knew they had to talk to Tere about that, I knew that Tere said something."

As if a fresh breeze had just entered The Tower and her soul, The Survivor Lois Fraley, is once again strong. She thinks about her interaction; *Yeah, Tere knows. I can do this. I can make it out of here.*

Later in the evening of Day Twelve, the telephone rings inside of The Tower. On the other end of the line is a radio newsman who has agreed to do the interview under certain conditions laid down by the Command Center and the State; these conditions state that the interview will not be played publicly until after Officer Fraley's peaceful release by the hostage takers. The following interview released by KTAR has been transcribed verbatim.

Wassenaar is all smiles as he listens to the newsman that he has requested for this interview, "….inside the Arizona State Prison Lewis Complex. The two inmates holding a female corrections officer hostage in the nation's longest prison standoff have asked to talk with 620 KTAR, and we are granting that request, as a condition for the release of the corrections officers, and for them to come out. We are talking with Ricky Wassenaar. Ricky."

115

"Yes."

"How did we get here?"

"Well, it's been a rocky road, but here we are."

The newsman asks, "What kind of rocky road was that?"

"Well, it was initially an escape attempt. We were on our way out. This was a stopping point to get some arms - to get some firearms to get out of here. Unfortunately, the plan went bad in The Tower and we were unable to make our way up front and secure our release, so to speak."

"Why stay at this tower for this long?"

"Well, we've had a few demands that were un-met. So, the negotiations have been slow and grinding out, and we haven't been asking for anything unreasonable. No helicopters, no, you know, million dollars, or none of that stuff, just the essentials, like blankets. So, uh, you know, we -- we're on concrete floors here, so . . . food for the officers - she's got medical conditions, she needs medication. We - it took us a while to get that done."

The interviewer asks for clarification, "So, we had an escape attempt that I guess went bad, as you put it?"

"Yes."

"We end up in this tower?"

"Yes."

"Where do we take it from there?"

Ricky minimizes his position, "Well, we only have one officer now."

"Right. Now, where do we – what happens here – from here on out?"

The convict begins to explain his view of the situation, "Well, it's - we have a few more steps to take, a few more negotiated steps, such as, you know, talking to family, speaking with family members. See, it's - it's - this is a Protective Segregated yard. They put me in Protective Segregation back in '97 when they received a letter saying that my life was in danger. I had spent eleven - over eleven years in the general population prior to that. There was no, no threat on my life, it was just, you know, somebody wanted me off the yard; possibly because he felt that I was a threat to him. And I guess this was when the Protective Segregation population was in a class action lawsuit against the State because it - against the Department, I should say, because the Department of Corrections was forcing the Protective Segregations back into general population."

"Ricky, just a moment ago you mentioned that you would like to talk to your family."
"I've – I've already spoken with my sister."
"Uh-huh."
"I, uh, have two sisters and a brother that flew down from Michigan here. But I would like to, you know, speak with my mother, who is back in Michigan. There's a few other requests that we would like to make. However, what I was getting to is I come to this yard, this Protective Segregation yard, and they treat everybody like… you know, it's… this yard is full of child molesters and low lifes and 99% of the populations are… they're dirt. They're the worst of the worst. And…and when they throw me in here with these people, these officers treat us like dirt constantly, with no respect. You know, this, uh - when they - when they poke - poke an animal in a cage long enough sooner or later he's going to find a way to open up that cage door."

The newsman attempts flattery, "Right. So, it sounds

like you're not like these fellow inmates --"

"No."

"-- so you're... you're not like... the type of person who wants to put anybody in danger. It sounds like you're the type of person that wants to... to find a way to settle all of this."

Wassenaar accepts the compliment, "Oh, that's... that's not what it... it's your opinion, that's not other people's opinion."

"What I was asking for is, for you to give your opinion about that."

Ricky loves when someone asks for his opinion, "Well, you know, I'm doing a long, long time in here. I'm more than likely going to die an old man in prison. The negotiator and I have set forth a few different steps, like... I believe there's like four steps, and this interview was one of them steps. I was, uh, I've been asking to speak with the media since Day One. Day Number One of this so-called, you know, Tower Takeover, or whatever the hell you want to call it, I've been asking to speak with the media. And they took, what is it, twelve days now, almost thirteen days, into our thirteenth day before they, you know, let me speak with a person from the media."

Wassenaar continues the conversation with a lie, "Every piece of the... I mean, they took thirty-one hours to get a handcuff key for their officers that I... that I gave them my word, and did, return back to them. You know, I mean, every step of this negotiation process is, uh, is - it's like pulling teeth. If they were so concerned about their officers, I think they would have sent a key immediately, for one. They were too worried about sending this radio and sending a battery charger, both of which had listening devices in 'em. They were both bugged. We had to break them open and remove the bugs."

The newsman cuts to the chase, "So, you want to resolve this, you want to settle this quickly?"

"Well, that was in my intention at the beginning, but they've showed that they, the Department of Corrections has showed very little interest in resolving anything quick... quickly. This could have been resolved days ago. The Department acts like they don't care about their employees."

"Okay. We have, you have as much time as you would like, so if something sounds, you know, don't feel you're under any pressure here to... to... that we're going to cut you off, or, you know, or anything. So, we do have the media interview. It will run on... on KTAR, I can assure you of that. Is this something that will help settle or resolve this?"

Ricky wants more air time, "I didn't really air all of my grievances. I wanted to."

"Okay."

"You know, say... about, you know, the... the way the staff treats people who are in here that don't want to be in here."

"All right."

"You know. I'm not talking about in prison, I'm talking about in... in Protective Segregation."

The interviewer attempts to redirect, "Right. Well, this is in Arizona. Let me ask you this, for you and Steven: I believe one of the conditions to settle this whole deal is to, to be transferred to another prison outside of the state of Arizona?"

"Yes."

"As I understand it, that can be, that can happen, and they can make that happen. If they make that happen, will you settle this?"

The Legal Beagle comes out in Wassenaar as he speaks, "Well, the thing is... is they're in a... it's a coercion situation. They, uh, according to the Arizona law, and law throughout the nation, is, uh, in a hostage situation the law enforcement can make any promises in writing or otherwise that they want. And because they're... it's... they're under duress because it's coercion, none of, none of them documents will hold up in a court of law. They will, uh..."

"Okay."

"They're not worth the paper they're printed on."

"Then..."

"But--"

"Go ahead."

Ricky does go ahead, "We would, we would be transferred with Federal Marshals to a Federal Holding Facility and then on to another state. However, you know, that's... like I said, the law, not worth the paper it's printed on, and will not hold up in court. We could not enforce that in a Court of Law and make them do that."

"Are you... are you going to take their offer?"

"We're, we're still debating that."

"What is to debate?"

The convict explains, "Well, it's... it's... what I explained and... but I kind of bet what the odds are... are... you know, when the odds are with me. Right now, the odds are not with me."

"What... what do you need?"

"I don't know, I can't answer that."

The radio newsman attempts flattery again, "As we started out in this interview, you did not strike me as a person who wants harm to come to another individual, and that was witnessed when you released the first Corrections Officer. Am I on the right track?"

"You know what, I don't wish that on anybody, but that's not my call right now, it's - it's what they're willing to honor. Are you going to send out over the air, as well, about the Interstate Compact?"

The interviewer is obviously flustered, "Yes, yes, we're going to... this is going to be-"

"About their... about"

An unenforceable promise is made to Ricky, "This will be aired in its entirety, is what I am trying to say, because that's part of the agreement that we're working under--"

"Right."

"-- with you."

"Okay."

"Before we wrap it up here, what will it take, Ricky --"

"Yes?"

"-- to settle this situation and have this woman released?

Suddenly the chameleon Ricky K Wassenaar changes color once again espousing a religious side, "It'll take a whole lot of praying to, uh, wherever you pray to, and a little bit of luck."

"If you hear this interview on the radio, will you... will you release -"

"That's a... a step that will be... this interview itself is a step that is one step closer to her release. This was a pre-requisite to her being released."

121

"All right, Ricky. Thank you very much for taking the time with 620 KTAR. We've been speaking from the Arizona State Prison Lewis Complex."

After the telephone interview, Wassenaar walks with a cocky strut as he paces The Tower's floor. In his mind he has won, he has beaten "The Man" by making the State of Arizona allow him to speak publicly about his and Steven Coy's plight and the promises that are being made to them.

Day Thirteen for Lois Fraley was more than just another hash mark carved into the paint with her small pencil stub. The radio station interview did not play as promised, and Wassenaar is becoming more and more irritable by the hour.

Let down by the administration once again, Lois realizes that her life can end at any moment, probably today. Not because of the actions of desperate men who did not hear the conditions of the interview correctly, but because of the purported broken promise between the negotiators, the radio station and the hostage takers.

Lois realizes the importance to Wassenaar that his radio interview be played unrestricted and in its entirety, not just for local audiences, but on a national level. She has heard Ricky and Coy speak for weeks now on the importance of having their words played publicly, forcing the entire administration to back into a corner, forcing them to honor their promise of the out-of-state transfers.

Realizing the content of his criticism of PSs during the interview, Wassenaar suddenly feels a need to "save face."

He realizes that he spoke at length about his disdain for protective segregation inmates and the fact that the Morey Unit Yard is full of child molesters and low lifes; the worst of the worst. However, the tired convict also realizes that "if you lay down with dogs, you get fleas."

His announcement to the world, if it ever plays was that ninety-nine percent of protective segregation inmates are scum. That means that in his own mind, Ricky K. Wassenaar is truly a one percenter and that Steven John Coy is not.

Coy is just another Rapo, and thanks to him, here they are, stuck in The Tower with no place to run.

Thinking back to his conversation on Day Seven with negotiators who tried to "divide and conquer" himself and Coy, Ricky has an idea. Maybe things would go better if it were just he and Lois.

If Wassenaar can have "the man" take Coy out of the picture with a single sniper's shot, then he would not have to worry about the company he keeps any longer.

On the morning of Day Thirteen, Wassenaar did try to do something about his partner, the "rapo," by discussing with a negotiator his desire to have Coy killed by TSU snipers in what will later be known as "The Whisper Conversation."

FBI Special Agent Dan Musser was the primary negotiator who took the call at 1012 hours on Day Thirteen. While whispering, Wassenaar explained the need for the authorities to kill Steven Coy sometime in the near future. Ricky told Agent Musser that Coy was not going to take "the deal" (out-of-state transfers), and was planning to kill Lois in an attempt to force the State of Arizona to seek the death penalty, the ultimate "Suicide by Cop."

This information was passed on at 1128 hours to Negotiator Ragsdale as he took over the position of primary negotiator from Musser.

Wassenaar is going to get Coy onto the Observation Deck of The Tower so that the snipers can kill him. Up to this point Coy had only been seen one other time, on Day One partially exposed in the hatch; so, unless he is set up by Wassenaar, there is not much of a likelihood of seeing Coy up there.

Wassenaar was true to his word. Coy *did go up* on the deck of The Tower for a short amount of time at 1248 hours, testing the steadfast nerves of the Sniper Teams once again as they attempt to, but cannot establish both targets for a simultaneous shot.

Later that day, Wassenaar walks on the Observation Deck while smoking a cigarette, once again "on scope" by snipers as the spotters search for Coy and the ability to end this thing in an instant with two well placed shots.

Ricky is angry about the water being turned off to The Tower as well as the fact that an entire day has passed since the radio interview was given, yet it still hasn't been played to the public. The miscreant feels cheated by the negotiators and the radio station; this is not acceptable.

Inside of The Tower Lois is tending to her chores of cleaning while the radio plays. Wassenaar climbs down into The Tower from above.

"Anything yet?" Wassenaar asks.

"Nope," Coy replies.

Ricky's face displays his displeasure; he is livid, "What kinda bullshit is that?"

Coy asks for clarification, "Rooster, did he say exactly

when they were gonna play it?"

The angry convict's reply is terse and snide, "I didn't bother to fucking ask."

After a day of fruitless discussions with negotiators concerning the radio interview, and the snipers refusal to kill Coy, Wassenaar pulls another unprecedented stunt for the tactical teams. At 1722 hours, he appears on the Observation Deck holding a shotgun backwards in his right hand. The hostage taker is attempting to display his bravado while still keeping the sniper teams in check.

The rules of engagement read "#4 One inmate appears with lethal force, non-threatening: Red Light, do not shoot."

Later in the NOC, the Primary Negotiator is speaking on the rescue phone, trying to appease the upset hostage taker about the interview, "I understand that Rick. No, Ricky that's not our fault. All we could do is "hook you guys up," and we did, didn't we?"

Wassenaar's voice is heard through headsets by other team members who listen in, "You guys fucked me. I trusted you, and you fucked me."

The negotiator continues to speak, "You can't put this on us, please don't put it on Lois………..You're right, I agree with you…….What?………Possibly, but let's not point fingers just yet……….Yeah, I know about fingers………No Ricky, I agree that this isn't good."

The trained communicator redirects the dissatisfied hostage taker, "Alright, hey, are you guys hungry? We have some meds to deliver to Lois, maybe we can bring you something……………What do you want to eat?………… Yeah, I like those too……..let me see what I can do."

When the Negotiations Team Leader walks into the

NOC, the Primary turns off the Rescue Phone and removes his headset showing his concern. "They're still mad about the interview not being played, but I've got them thinking with their stomachs again, get me some cinnamon rolls; and find out about that interview."

On Day Fourteen at 1536 hours more negotiated items are delivered to The Tower. These include three cinnamon rolls, one bottle of Pedialite for Lois' medical condition, one bottle of Gatorade and one pack of cigarettes.

After fourteen days of negotiations, resolution seems near; Wassenaar and Coy are apparently going to consider taking the State at "its word" that the out-of-state transfers will be honored.

However, when the radio station interview did not play as promised, Wassenaar became more and more irritable. In a letter that was written to Arizona Republic Reporter Dennis Wagner, Wassenaar expressed his sentiment:

The interview was supposed to be part of the agreed negotiations, and was supposed to be played the following day. When it wasn't, I told them all that I wanted that interview retracted as part of the broken agreement, and did not want it played at anytime in the future. Several inmates have since told me that they heard the interview. That interview was attained by their broken negotiated promises! I would like to sue their asses! For ADC to deny the media access, was to extend the situation to 15 days, when it could have been over in a couple of days.

All we really wanted the news media for, was to broadcast the agreements that we made, Out-of-State Incarceration, so that they may have a little difficulty reneging on the agreements.

Chapter Fifteen
Just Another Day

As the sun rises over The Tower on Day Fifteen of the longest hostage siege in United States prison history, Lois Fraley realizes that this is just another day; like all of the others that have preceded it.

Dirty beams of light shine through peepholes cut into the blacked out windows illuminating dust motes in the filthy tower. Garbage is scattered everywhere; fast food containers, pizza cartons, and soft drink containers attract swarms of flies that buzz above the floor which is strewn with cigarette butts and hundreds of insect carcasses. Lois' housekeeping chores have been lacking of late, as she truly is not feeling well. Her bones hurt and her joints ache. She has a high fever that makes her very thirsty, but the water in The Tower is putrid and stagnant, and the soda pop is too sweet to quench her thirst.

In a corner, Coy snores as Wassenaar sits propped up against the desk also asleep. Lois tosses and turns as it is getting even harder for her to rest on the concrete floor of The Tower. Her hips and knees continue to ache as there is no padding at all beneath her.

Eight long lonely days have drug by slowly since Jason's release. Lois finds herself really missing him; she feels so isolated. At least when Jason was here she could lay her head on his legs or lap for comfort.

The uncertainty of the moment and the lack of sleep are taking their toll on this once strong woman. Lois begins to drift back into sleep, and then in a heartbeat she is jolted awake by fear when Coy suddenly stops snoring. She settles back into sadness when, instead of rising, the hostage taker only tosses in his sleep. The Survivor Lois Fraley begins to pray once again, thinking of her daughter Kyla while trying to reaffirm herself.

"Lord, I'm sad. I don't think that these guys want to kill me, but it doesn't matter whether I live or die. I may not be the best Mom in the world, but I know that Kyla loves me. If I ever……..no, when I get out of this, I'm going to smother that girl with love."

Later that morning, Lois looks disheveled and weary as she sits listening to the radio. Coy holds the shotgun while Wassenaar rises and goes to each window in The Tower to peer out through the small peep holes. Wassenaar notices that Lois does not look good as she mouths words in a muted prayer, *"….on earth as it is in heaven give us our daily bread..."*

"Lois, you okay?" Wassenaar asks.

"What do you think?"

"You don't look so good."

Lois is sick and tired of being sick and tired, "Gee, ya think? Ricky, what did I ever do to Y'all? I'll tell you what, nothing. Do you think that I deserve this? No, I don't. I am so close to just pissing you off so that you do shoot me, just to end this thing."

Wassenaar and Coy cannot believe their ears. They are both in disbelief.

She continues, "I am really at a point where I think I'd rather be dead right now. I come to work to make money to feed me and my family, and what happens? You show up mad at the world, and take your shit out on me."

Her anger becomes a challenge, "Come on Ricky, you guys keep talking about not caring whether you live or die;

prove it. Why don't you just shoot me, so that they can come in here and put you out of your misery?"

Wassenaar's apology seems sincere, "Hey, I'm sorry I asked."

In a later interview Lois shared her depression and despair at the uncertainty of her situation, *"Everyday was a low point, because it was a day I was not around my family, my child, my partner, it was not knowing if one day I was going to live, the next day I was dead."*

At 0920 hours on Day Fifteen another demand is satisfied. Coy is on the telephone listening to the negotiator on the other side of the line who speaks, "Okay Steven. We've got your Uncle Bob here, and he wants to talk to you, but we need a little something from you. We need to hear that you guys are willing to work with us here."

The hostage taker is calm and pleasant as he speaks optimistically, "I think that we're very close to resolving this. I just really need to talk with him one last time, I love the man. He was more of a father to me than his brother, my real dad. I have a feeling that we can work this thing out together, I just need to hear it from someone that I can trust, and that's my Uncle Bob."

The negotiator prepares for the Third Person Intermediary, "Alright, I'm going to put you through."

Across the prison compound, inside of a room near the NOC, Steven Coy's Uncle Bob is seated holding a telephone at a table with a negotiation team member next to him monitoring the TPI's conversation. There are notes and paperwork in front of both. After being connected to his errant nephew, Uncle Bob speaks, "Steven? Good, I need to talk to you."

Later on the morning of Day Fifteen, Lois re-awakens to find that Coy has a smile on his face while he is on the telephone finishing his conversation with Uncle Bob. Wassenaar stands nearby with a wide grin on his heavily stubbled face. Lois senses that something is different; the hostage takers seem to be pleased with something that must have occurred while she was sleeping.

After Coy hangs up the phone he seems pleased, "Good deal."

Almost gleeful, Wassenaar is interested, "Really? What did your Uncle Bob have to say?"

"Well here's the deal...."

Before Coy can expound on his conversation, Wassenaar stops him and then issues a directive to Lois, "Hold on. Lois, lay down on the floor and hum 'cause me and Pony have to talk."

Officer Fraley does as she is told and lies down on the filthy tower floor where she begins to do as she was ordered, all the while thinking about what has started off as just another day has the possibility of becoming a really great day. It occurs to Lois that it is probably the fact that the hostage takers have spoken with their loved ones that might bring this siege to an end.

In her mind her hums become like mantras as they become a musical prayer, *"God, please let me see my loved ones."*

During an interview after her release Lois explained the feeling of the morning of her last day as a hostage.

"I didn't know until that...until this morning. As I woke up, and I guess that they had been up for a little bit, or at least Ricky was. And he told me to lay down and hum. And whenever they wanted to have a private conversation, that's what they did. And I think that he finally convinced

Pony that you know, 'Don't do this in front of your Dad (Uncle Bob), and you know, 'I wouldn't do this in front of my sister.'

At 1004 hours the NOC is busy as negotiators work with their Team Leader to prepare for a peaceful resolution by formulating a surrender plan that will bring everyone out safely; hostage and hostage takers. The Primary is on the telephone talking to Wassenaar, bartering with the hostage taker.

"Alright Ricky, here's the deal. We put Coy's Uncle Bob on the phone, but you have got to do something for us. Rick, we've gone beyond two weeks into this thing, and it's time to end it. Let's end it today."

The negotiator listens to Wassenaar's response, and then interjects, "I know that this has got to be wearing on you too. Lois is in there getting sicker, yes or no? Okay and I believe that you don't want anything to happen to her, but you've got to walk the walk man. I know that you can talk the talk. But let's see if you can walk the walk."

Negotiation team members listen in earnest while the Primary speaks, "What do you say?.....Alright,.....Yeah, possibly."

And then it appears as though a major development has occurred; Wassenaar and Coy have decided that they will discuss surrender, but only if it can be with Negotiator Ragsdale.

The Secondary Negotiator listens to Wassenaar's latest demand as concern shows on the face of the Primary who speaks, "Man, I just don't know about that. He lives all the way across the Valley, Rick. Oh, I do understand that, but this is rush hour and I can't move the traffic, can I?"

The negotiator promises to try his best to accommodate Wassenaar, who may just get his helicopter after all, "Sure we do. Let me get back to you."

The Primary turns off the Rescue Phone and then looks directly at his Secondary, "What do you think?"

"Well you heard it. He sounded sincere didn't he?"

"Yeah, we'd better get a 'page' out to Ragsdale."

Wassenaar is asking that his favorite and most trusted hostage negotiator, Bob Ragsdale, be the one that he and Coy "seal the deal" with when they talk about their final terms for surrender and a peaceful resolution. Ricky also demands that the power and water be turned back on in The Tower, so that they will have access to the bathroom and sink. He also wants his and Coy's property packed up, removed from their cells, and placed in a transport van. In addition, he wants four packs of cigarettes that are to be delivered to them prior to discussing their surrender.

To those in the NOC and the Command Center, it looks as if today might just be "the day," but only if things are done now, and done right. It has happened before; negotiators feel as though they have been close to peaceful resolution for days, only to have Coy and Wassenaar talk each other out of it. Since Coy has spoken with his uncle, it seems as though he and Wassenaar have decided to accept conditions, and are resigned to their surrender. Negotiators must move forward to make this thing happen, to bring Officer Fraley home.

Inside of The Tower, Wassenaar speaks intently into the telephone discussing his demands with a look that is mixed with resignation and surrender, "Compared to us coming out of The Tower, these demands are nothing. I'm not going to go back on my word. You get the power and water turned back on, get us some cigarettes, and you get

Bob Ragsdale here, meet some more of our minor demands and we're coming out."

Hearing these words, Lois' mood has changed from one of dread and uncertainty to a feeling of joy. It is as if the entire weight of the world is beginning to lift.

Coy also seems to be experiencing positive feelings that the ordeal will be ending soon. Lois understands that Uncle Bob has been, and still may be, instrumental in the surrender negotiations. Lois has been "working" Coy ever since Jason left eight days earlier. She has actually enjoyed making him discuss his family and his children, as he would listen to her talk about Kyla.

Gradually, Coy opens up to Lois, revealing interesting information about their last day by explaining the motive for her possible release to her, "The only reason that we're giving up is because my Uncle Bob is here. That's the only reason why were letting you go Lois."

Officer Fraley is grateful to finally hear the words that she has been wanting to hear for fifteen long days, but she also realizes that it is the agreement that the authorities have made with the hostage takers for the out-of-state transfers that will make or break the deal.

Lois' response to the good news is guarded as she shares her own feelings and concerns about her lack of faith and trust for the authorities, "Yeah, well it's not over yet Pony, I got a feeling that if Rooster doesn't screw this whole thing up, the fucking negotiators will."

And then, as a stipulation for their demands, Officer Fraley is allowed to speak with the Primary negotiator. Her voice is matter-of-fact, but weary, "This is Fraley, yeah I'm fine."

In the Negotiations Operations Center, the team also listens as Officer Fraley expresses her concerns with negotiators, "Please don't screw this up."

Meanwhile, across the vast expanse of Phoenix, a Department of Public Safety helicopter lands at a small grassy park that is adjacent to a nearby golf course in Bob Ragsdale's neighborhood. Bob is airlifted and expedited across the state with the intent and hope of "sealing the deal" with the hostage takers for their surrender. The fact that they specifically asked for him to negotiate the resolution is a good sign that indicates they are ready to end Lois' nightmare without violence.

At 1104 hours Wassenaar and Coy win their first victory, when they receive four packs of cigarettes that are delivered to The Tower. The hostage takers realize that these may be the last "smokes" that they will appreciate before they are forced to surrender "cold turkey."

At 1120 hours, Detective Robert Ragsdale enters the NOC where he is greeted by the Primary Negotiator, "Well, look what the cat drug in."
"Sorry to cut in like this."
The Primary removes his head set and hands it to Bob, "What? Are you kidding me? I want you to have this thing. I'm kind of happy that it's you, not me."
"Yeah, lucky me, I guess."
The Secondary continues to monitor the phone line while the Primary offers a sincere compliment, "No, seriously Bob, if any one can get Lois out of there safely, it's you. Make us proud Brother."
After donning the Rescue Phone's headset, Primary Hostage Negotiator Ragsdale looks at the two hand-writ-

ten notes that are still hanging in the NOC, *"Time is on our Side"* and *"Peaceful Resolution."*

He smiles, "Alright, lets do this thing."

Inside of The Tower, the telephone rings at 1129 hours. It is answered by Wassenaar, "Yeah, is that you Bob?"

After yesterdays "walk the walk and talk the talk" speech with Wassenaar, the H/Ts' resolution demands all seem pretty workable, with the exception of one, they are:

1. The electric power and water is to be turned back on, to allow them access to the Lower Tower bathroom.
2. To talk with Wassenaar's sister Rhonda.
3. To hear a recorded message from Coy's ex-wife.
4. Both inmates' personal property is to be placed in a transport van, which is to be parked close to The Tower.
5. Verified paperwork confirming that there will be no future incarceration in ADC or Maricopa County for future court proceedings.
6. Clothing.
7. Three Steaks, three baked potatoes, a twelve-pack of Heineken beer.

Of these demands most are considered "comfort items" and are allowable, all except for the last; the beer. It is a solid non negotiable, as well as a "no-brainer" in hostage negotiations, that you do not provide alcohol to already volatile gunmen. This is unheard of, and in Bob Ragsdale's eleven years of negotiations experience, this is only the second time that it has ever been requested. He knows that getting this demand past the Command Center will be virtually impossible.

It appears as though the Negotiations Team will have to

barter with two entities now, the Hostage Takers and the Command Center.

At 1152 hours the ultimate decision maker, Governor Janet Napolitano, arrives at the Command Center to assist Director Dora Schriro in resolving this incident peacefully. While Command is working through the demands, Negotiator Ragsdale speaks with and keeps the hostage takers, who seem quite reasonable, talking. There appears to be light at the end of this two week tunnel for Officer Fraley.

From the Command Center, the answer concerning the demand for alcohol is an emphatic "no." Negotiator Ragsdale was expecting this result, as he knows that Command is adamant about policy. Now, however, the negotiations team must barter within their own bureaucracy through communication with their Team Leader, who is stationed in the Command Center with the "Suits." The Command Center is also hesitant to restore electrical power to The Tower, which is beginning to become a major issue with Wassenaar.

At 1235 hours, inside of The Tower, Wassenaar scores his second victory. The negotiation team contacts the hostage takers and plays a recording from the former Mrs. Coy pleading for her ex-husband to give up and come out alive alongside Lois. In return, the hostage takers are supposed to allow Lois to go up onto the Observation Deck, one last time, for another visual wellness check, or better yet, the initiation of a tactical rescue.

Outside of The Tower, spotters, snipers and entry teams listen through their earphones to the TSU team leader speaking over the radio, "All teams, be advised that command is working on a surrender option with the H/Ts. Do not stand down; be prepared for command shot, countdown shot and entry. Realize that this is #2 at risk."

The teams acknowledge individually.

The "number two at risk" the team leader is referring to, is the fact that *the resolution phase is the second most dangerous of the four phases of any hostage taking incident.* Things can get ugly at any time throughout the carefully choreographed surrender process. Until safely restrained and led away to be identified, all involved parties are still considered to be potential adversaries.

At 1251 hours Wassenaar climbs through the access hatch to make another venture up onto the Observation Deck. Snipers and spotters watch through their scopes as Wassenaar pulls himself up onto the deck.

Radio traffic between the other four "hides" is intense, "Team Three, We are 'on scope' with Target One."

"Copy, Team Five is on scope with the hatch."

A team leader's voice announces to all involved, "Prepare for entry."

The entry team "stacks up" one behind the other, with a hand on the shoulder of the man in front of them for proximity and communication. The rescue ladder is ready to go, the demolitions team member holds the detonation switch.

Above the entry team, on the Observation Deck, a head pokes up through The Tower's hatch, initiating another tactical command issued to the sniper teams, "That's Fraley. Stand down on the hatch. Red light on the hatch."

As Lois climbs up further from below, she stops, then stares out across the rooftops, she sees a sniper and a spotter in their "hide" observing her through optical lenses. Suddenly her hopes and spirits are lifted when the man with the rifle looks up from his intent aim to give her a "thumbs up" signal.

The Survivor Lois Fraley realizes that *this is not just another day;* everything is going to be okay. The sniper and spotter watch as Lois radiates her happiness by smiling towards the marksmen.

Chapter Sixteen
Lois' Super Sunday

At 1326 hours on Feburary 01, 2004, prior to the beginning of Super Bowl XXXVIII, Ricky Wassenaar scores a victory of his own with the administration when he answers the telephone to find that his sister Rhonda is waiting on the other end of the line with a negotiator.

Wassenaar speaks with the negotiator, "Talk to me.... yeah, put her on.... Hi Rhonda Baby......Yeah, it's me, I've been thinking a lot about what you said, you know,...... Yeah, me too."

After the telephone conversation with his sister ends, the hostage taker seems calm. Rhonda has spoken to him twice now, and he feels much more positive about the state's promise of the out-of-state transfers for himself and Coy. It comes down to the fact that Ricky K. Wassenaar trusts his sister Rhonda Krenz.

Later, Wassenaar speaks at length with Negotiator Ragsdale concerning the request for twelve beers and the Command Center's steadfast refusal to provide them. Wassenaar comes up with a suggestion, "We'd settle for a six-pack. I'm not an alcoholic; I just want a couple of last beers."

After nearly two hours of negotiations, Bob Ragsdale has reduced the hostage takers demand down to three beers each and a couple of sodas. He sends the request up the chain-of-command to the administrators.

In the NOC the debate continues between the Negotiation Team Leader and The Primary Negotiator, who has a good point. Along with alcohol, weapons are also non-negotiable items. To Bob Ragsdale the irony of the situation is that hostage takers aren't supposed to have weapons or drugs either, but in The Tower they have both.

Bob offers to barter with Wassenaar some more with the intent of talking him down to one beer each.

The Negotiation Team Leader is concerned, but offers Ragsdale support, "I'll tell you Bob, Command is not real receptive to our idea. So, you want me to pitch one beer each and the power back on, right?"

The seasoned negotiator cannot help but comment on the irony of the offer, "Yeah boss, but you tell Command; one hostage, two suspects, a bunch of weapons, a tower and an entire prison for two beers; not bad."

As Wassenaar and Coy barter for beers in The Tower, 4,100 other convicts within the Arizona Prison Complex Lewis have been cheated out of what in prisons throughout the nation is an even more sacred day than Christmas; Super Bowl Sunday.

Super Bowl Sunday in male dominant institutions is a religious holiday of its own celebrated by its captive audiences who fill dayrooms and cells to enjoy the game.

Prisoners prepare for the day long in advance by ordering extra "commissary" from the institution's inmate stores. Extra bags of chips and liter bottles of carbonated beverages are shared and consumed during the festive six-hour event which includes pre and post game shows, commercials, the half time show, and the girls who stand on the sidelines cheering the opposing teams.

Inmates in their cells yell out to others throughout the

game. At times the prisons' tiers and dayrooms go silent, at other times they suddenly break out into cheers or profanity depending on which team you're rooting for or betting on.

On the day of the game, plastic garbage bags filled with "pruno" are removed from hiding places that have stored the homemade alcohol for days or even weeks while it ferments. Pruno is a very powerful prison wine often made from fruit, sugar and ketchup. It is so potent that two gallons can be a virtual liquor store, providing enough good cheer to get ten to twelve prisoners extremely drunk as they choke down the putrid concoction, sometimes while holding their noses.

Sports viewing and betting are common in prison, even though currency is not allowed. Well run pools are kept on "boards", which are small betting slips that are considered by staff to be contraband. Bets are often covered with commissary orders, drugs and even sex, postage stamps are also used as currency. It's not uncommon for an inmate with nothing to wager to offer to have to shave his entire body, eyebrows included, for picking the wrong team in a championship game.

As an after effect, an interesting phenomenon occurs each year shortly after the game is played; there is a sudden migration of the offenders from the general population who ask to be placed in Protective Segregation. To "honorable convicts" this is considered to be a disgrace, bankruptcy of yourself when you owe too much to too many.

On this day however, there will be no game enjoyed due to the television blackout that was initiated on Day One of the Morey Tower Takeover. And isn't it ironic that the two inmates that have screwed the rest of the institution out of this festive event are from Protective Segregation?

In the NOC, negotiators realize that what has started off as a good day, with the potential to become a great day, has just taken a turn for the worse. Wassenaar is angry because the power is still not on.

It is his intention to surrender, but only under his own terms; he is a very particular man and cleanliness is a necessity in his life. The "Tower Takeover" is now in its fifteenth day, but it has been longer still since Ricky or anyone else in The Tower has had a shower or a shave. If, and when he does surrender, he will only go in fresh clothing, brushed teeth and combed hair.

Along with the Command Center's steadfast refusal to supply beer, they continue to be reticent about restoring electrical power to The Tower. This decision does not set well with the fastidious Ricky K. Wassenaar.

At 1355 hours Ragsdale speaks on the phone once again with Wassenaar concerning the power. While trying to "seal the deal" for the surrender, the primary negotiator has been tasked with an impossible request from the command center; they want Ragsdale to convince the hostage takers to throw their weapons up onto the Observation Deck before the power will be restored. Only minutes after this is relayed to Wassenaar, things get ugly fast.

On the day of her release Lois shared the tension of this moment that she heard by eavesdropping on the negotiations: *"Today, the negotiator Bob said that the only way that they were willing to turn on the electricity, is if they (Coy and Wassenaar) threw the guns up top, or something like that. Well needless to say, that pissed off Ricky."*

In The Tower at 1409 hours Wassenaar does get "pissed off" and then seems to lose it when he hears the suggestion of disarmament.

With anger and disbelief, the incensed convict screams into the telephone's handset, "Really?? You've got to be shitting me! What is their fucking problem??

The irate hostage taker does not wait for an answer before he continues with a barrage of continuous threats. He screams, "Yeah, well you tell them that this is directly from Ricky K. Fucking Wassenaar: *"They can take the electricity and shove it up their asses and the phone will be off for 24 hours, and I'll have a new demand, and they'll have eight hours to fill that, and if they don't fill it, then the phone will be off for another 48 hours."*

In the NOC, Negotiator Ragsdale is extremely concerned when he hears Wassenaar's ultimate threat concerning the end of the siege.

In a more controlled voice and demeanor, the convict issues another ultimatum, "I am five seconds from shutting you down, and not talking to anybody for two days. I want the power back on, I want access to the bathroom, and I want it now."

Ricky K Wassenaar wants things his way, and he wants them right now. His antisocial view of his little world in The Tower and the attention that he has brought to his and Coy's situation is classic.

The telephone line abruptly goes dead; the conversation has been terminated by the hostage taker. Wassenaar has just thrown a "fit" and now the Command Center must make a decision.

The decision to turn the electrical power back on to The Tower was made and initiated "post haste." At 1439 hours, exactly one-half of an hour after his demand, Ricky K. Wassenaar scores his fourth victory, but only for a moment. Shortly after it was turned on, the power was once again extinguished, sending the hostage taker into another tirade.

Wassenaar is once again livid. Lois trembles with fear while she and Coy listen to the escalating dialogue become rant and rage. Wassenaar snaps and begins to scream into the telephone at Bob Ragsdale again, "Yeah, well you want to play Mother Fuckers?? Here you go! You ready for this?? Let's see how your trained killers handle this one!"

Ragsdale overhears Wassenaar order Coy to be prepared, "Pony you hear a shot, you kill her! I'm going up!"

At 1446 hours the irate convict grabs the 37 mm. projectile launcher and scrambles up onto the Observation Deck, while Coy picks up the AR-15 and points it at Lois' face. "I got your back Rooster!"

Radio traffic is rampant as sniper and spotter teams are once again sent into the Red Zone with less than a second's notice. They've identified the threat and are poised and ready to take out the man with the weapon, yet the Green Light order is never issued, even after Ricky fires a cartridge of baton rounds into the Yard.

The TSU Commander issues the order via radio, "Stand down. Red Light. Repeat, Stand down. Red Light."

Inside of The Tower Lois is incredulous, yet angry once again. She cannot believe how prophetic her earlier comment was concerning Ricky, he is going to jeopardize her release. This is supposed to be Officer Fraley's last day of captivity, yet she waits for the sniper's shot to sound making hers the next imminent death at the hands of Steven John Coy.

Lois shared her feelings about Wassenaar's antics shortly after her release: *"I was waiting for the snipers to shoot him. It just about pissed me off. I'm fixing to go home and he's fixing to play around with these guns. Boy, if I would have been able to take that shotgun, it would have been the end of him (Wassenaar). Screw with my ride home."*

Wassenaar's tirade has caused all involved to become concerned. How can they successfully negotiate a peaceful resolution with the convict when he can go from calm, cool and collected, and ready to surrender one moment, to the volatile, explosive person that he has just shown himself to be?

Negotiator Ragsdale realizes that no matter who is responsible for something going wrong during a negotiation, the hostage taker usually lashes out at the person that he considers culpable for the misfortune of a wrong decision. Usually, it's the one individual that is supposed to be an ally, and that is the negotiator.

Hostage Negotiators are special men and women, who like snipers, have also endured an intensive battery of testing and interviews. The criterion for selection is someone who is a "cool thinker" that can keep their own head, while others around them seem to be losing theirs.

Detective Ragsdale is a fine example of what a negotiator should be in this world of saving lives through dialogue. His patience, kindness and knowledge of the human psyche is what makes him what he is, the epitome of the time honored phrase, "The Negotiator."

The good news within the NOC is that this negotiator was a successful intermediary between Wassenaar, Coy and Command with Officer Fraley's best interests as his primary concern; he has gotten Command to acquiesce by getting them to approve one beer each for the hostage takers.

This is also good news within The Tower. Ricky knows that while men and women throughout the United States sit back to enjoy the New England Patriots challenge the Carolina Panthers in Super Bowl XXXVIII, Ricky K. Wassenaar and Steven John Coy will be able to feel like "free men" as they enjoy a steak and a beer.

At 1513 hours what negotiators hope will be the final delivery is taken to The Tower. As agreed, Wassenaar and Coy receive the updated and revised paperwork for their out-of-state transfers, along with fresh inmate uniforms consisting of shirts, pants, underwear, socks and shoes. Along with these items are what may very well be the last good food and drink that the hostage takers may ever enjoy; three steaks, three baked potatoes, three sodas and two twelve-ounce cans of beer.

After their dinner at 1618 hours, Wassenaar speaks almost apologetically into the phone with Bob Ragsdale discussing the deliveries that have already been made, "Yeah, things are a lot better on this side too. It was ugly for a while, I agree. So, I have the papers and the clothing. I'm feeling a lot cleaner now. Man, I have no idea how those homeless guys can handle it. I know I couldn't."

Ricky continues, "I'll tell you what. We've got a couple

of more hours left, so how about I give you a call at say, around 5:30 to discuss the particulars...Okay good, ...yeah, you can call here. It doesn't matter."

At 1623 hours sniper teams are once again poised at the ready to take any necessary shot to end the siege when Inmate Coy's head unexpectedly "pops" up out of the Observation Deck's access hatch. The second hostage taker peers through a pair of binoculars as he watches members of the Bureau of Prisons staged on the perimeter of The Tower's base.

Inside of the NOC, Bob Ragsdale places a phone call to The Tower at 1716 hours. It is answered by Coy who advises him, "Call back later, you're early."
Realizing that he has placed the call before the agreed upon time, the primary negotiator agrees and then calls back fifteen minutes later with the intention of talking through the surrender process specifics.
Once again, Coy answers, this time advising Ragsdale to, "Call back later, we're busy."

Another call is placed from the NOC at 1745 hours, again it is met with a refusal by Coy to connect the negotiator with Wassenaar.

Inside of the command center as well as inside of the NOC, staff members are not happy with Wassenaar's broken promise and cessation of communication; this is a bad sign. Have the authorities been significantly "worked" by the con men in The Tower who have eaten a nice meal while enjoying alcoholic beverages provided by the Great State of Arizona? Do the hostage takers intend to draw this siege out longer?

Finally, at approximately 1748 hours the Rescue Phone in the NOC rings. The primary negotiator answers, "This is Ragsdale."

On the other end, Ricky Wassenaar speaks, "You ready to do this thing Bob?"

Pleased, Bob replies, "I know we are, Ricky. How about you guys?"

The convict's voice sounds weary, "Yeah, we're almost ready."

Negotiator Ragsdale is pleased, but still apprehensive, "Okay, good. We need to discuss and agree on the basics of the surrender process. Rick, we want everyone out of there safe."

After discussing the specifics, and agreeing upon a surrender time of 1830 hours, Wassenaar proclaims that his word is solid, "You got my word, we three are coming out today."

"And I believe you Rick; I'll see you when you come out."

After terminating the call with the push of a button, Negotiator Ragsdale looks towards the secondary negotiator and makes a comment, "I hope this is it."

As stated earlier, the second most dangerous time of any hostage situation is the Resolution Phase, even when it is successfully negotiated to surrender. That is why all tactical team members involved need to be informed; snipers and spotters, entry teams, arrest teams, perimeter security and all outside law enforcement agencies.

Of utmost concern is that the hostage takers understand exactly what is expected of them and that they not vary or deviate from the surrender ritual in any way. The command center demands that all involved parties are aware, informed and "singing from the same sheet," so to speak.

The duty of disseminating this information is now the responsibility of Bob Ragsdale, who must express to Wassenaar and Coy that the security and safety of the hostage and the hostage takers is paramount. The goal is that everyone comes out alive.

This logic for some is tough to swallow. Most uniformed and plain clothes officers involved could care less what happens to Ricky K. Wassenaar and Steven John Coy, the two malcontents who have just held a fellow officer against her will for the last two weeks.

These "brothers and sisters of the badge" risk their lives every day to keep our communities safe from the very kind of people that have taken the female officer hostage. Wassenaar and Coy have held Lois Fraley hostage for over 350 hours, and done God-knows-what to her for fifteen days and fourteen nights. Are her fellow officers and the people in tactical gear angry?

Yes and rightfully so, but these men and women are professionals who don't act on the grudges that they may hold. Regardless of their emotions, they control their actions and do not act with reprisal. That is the difference between the Keepers and the Kept.

At 1817 hours on Day Fifteen, the sniper teams are not surprised, but pleased to see Wassenaar climb up onto the Observation Deck dressed in prison issued orange coveralls.

They know that "Ricky in Orange" is a signal for the officials and the tactical teams to know that the agreed upon surrender ritual is ready to begin, and that The Tower's door is clear for opening by the tactical teams. Wassenaar realizes that he is still "under the gun" by the sniper teams and has let it be known to negotiators that he is prepared at any moment for death or surrender.

As he climbs back down into The Tower Ricky asks Coy, "Well Pony, you ready to do this?"
"Yeah, I guess so."
The question is asked of Officer Fraley next, "Lois, how 'bout you?"
The concerned woman replies without much emotion, "I'm scared."
Wassenaar can't believe his ears. What does Lois Fraley have to fear?
He asks her, "Why's that? You're going home Lois, and we're not. You have everything to look forward to and we have nothing. What are you afraid of Lois?"
Lois speaks matter-of-factly, "You Ricky, and you Pony. 'Cause it's not over until it's over."

These are some pretty intuitive words from the female officer who has been kidnapped, beaten, raped and starved to the point of wanting to die. Sure, it's not over until she is safely in the hands of the tactical team members, but will it really be over then? Will it ever truly be over for The Survivor Lois Fraley?
Probably not.

This traumatic incident will most likely shadow Lois for the rest of her natural life. At best, she will come to grips with what happened and try to deal with it. However, the haunting memory and nightmare of fifteen days as the lone "pig" trapped in a house of bricks, held by two lone wolves, who huffed and puffed and found their way into the Morey Unit Guard Tower, will remain within her life forever. But for now, it's just time to go.

At 1820 hours inside of the NOC, negotiators watch the live video "feed" as the Bureau of Prison's tactical team approach The Tower door and then props it open with a sandbag. The team safely retreats approximately ten yards into the shadows.

At the top of the spiral staircase, Wassenaar and Coy smoke what may be their last cigarettes as what they consider themselves to be, "free men." They stand with Lois, who is unrestrained and ready to go home. Coy hangs the removed belly chains onto a rack that is attached to the top of the stairs.

She wonders, "Is this it, is it over? Am I really going home?"

One thing that Officer Fraley is certain of is that it's not over until it's over. During the last two weeks she has seen a wide variety of emotions and mental states expressed from these two malcontents, and she is aware that anything can change at any time, without a moment's notice.

That fear soon compounds itself into reality when Coy does something that is not a part of the carefully choreographed surrender plan; he picks up the 12-guage shotgun and stands directly by Lois, while her mind runs wild with thoughts of freedom; so close and yet so far away.

Lois asks with concern, "What's that for Pony?"

The reply is matter-of-fact, "It's for you Lois, if you try anything."

Lois' veins run cold once again as she feels the blood rushing through her body with what may very well be her last time to experience "fight or flight" in her life.

Officer Fraley tries to calm the hostage taker, "You

don't need it, you guys have won, and you're moving out of state soon."

Coy's eyes narrow as he points the barrel at Lois' head and then comments, "I'll fucking do it Lois."

The tired, hungry, dirty officer feels as though there is no hope left of ever seeing Kyla or Tere again, "I know you will."

Lois' legs seem to turn into cement as she watches Ricky Wassenaar begin to descend the spiral staircase. Coy nudges her with the butt of the shotgun, causing Lois to begin the treacherous descent.

The stairs are narrow, cheaply built and not designed for the weight of three large people at once. As they descend, the staircase begins to move left to right causing the hanging belly chains above them to rattle.

When they reach the "blacked out" base of The Tower, a bright light from outside illuminates the only exit point, The Tower's door.

At 1825 hours on Day Fifteen of the longest hostage siege in US Prison history, Ricky K. Wassenaar comes out of The Tower with his hands up. As the Arrest Team advances, they issue a directive to the hostage taker who complies with the order by turning around and lying on the ground where he is restrained.

Lois is ready to walk into the warm, bright, guiding light and the fresh air that is freedom; anything is better than where she has been. Her mind races with pleasurable thoughts, and then she realizes that Coy may have placed the shotgun down, but he is only three feet behind her.

The Survivor Lois Fraley forgoes the negative thought, takes a long deep breath and then walks forward into the light as she exits The Tower. She is greeted by two TSU members who are assigned her rescue. They reach out to her, and clasp onto her upper arms with solid but gentle support. As the men whisk Officer Fraley away to salvation, she cannot believe it, she's free.

In her own words after her release, Lois spoke of the last few moments in The Tower and the uncertainty of the surrender, "I didn't know if I was going to live or die till the minute I walked out of there."

After Lois is escorted away, Coy exits The Tower and is taken into custody by an Arrest Team Member after being taken down to the ground with a comment, "Get on the ground fucker."
The Rapist Steven John Coy comments, "Hey, you don't have to make this personal."
"Really?"

Inside of the NOC, the incident recorder makes one final log entry, "1828 hours. Coy out, cuffed. All in custody. Incident over. Amen."

At 1832 hours, as Officer Fraley is placed onto a medical gurney for transport by helicopter to a nearby hospital, she is approached and greeted with a kind touch and a genuine smile as she feels a soft hand squeeze her own. This show of affection and endearment comes from the kind but tough woman who has spent many hours in the command center working diligently for Lois' freedom. Dora Schriro is the woman who worked together with the Department of Corrections and the entire State of Arizona to bring this officer home.

Afterword

Since 2004, the question has been asked by many people who have expressed interest in this epic story, "Where are they now? What happened after Lois Fraley was released, and Coy and Wassenaar were arrested?"

The state of Arizona did take this event personally. It cost over 3.6 Million dollars for the safe release of Officers Lois Fraley and Jason Auch.

The truth of the matter is that the two inadequate inmates who were cornered like rats while trying to escape, have been treated fairly by a system that is run by the very type of people that they held hostage.

After surrendering into the hands of the Federal Bureau of Prisons both convicts were immediately transferred to the Maricopa County jail, which is run by the infamous Sheriff Joe Aeropio, Arizona's "get tough" lawman. It was there that the hostage takers got a taste of the hard-line approach of the special security measures and procedures that were set into place to prevent a repeat of The Tower incident.

While in court the rapist Steven John Coy decided to accept responsibility for his part, as he "took his medicine" by pleading guilty to kidnapping, assault, sexual assault and other charges. He is now serving seven consecutive life terms in Maine under the agreement that was reached with negotiators during the siege.

On the other hand by pleading not guilty, Ricky K. Wassenaar once again stayed as true to his colors as a chameleon can be, while revealing more evidence of his antisocial tendencies.

He accepts no responsibility for the event, much less the sexual assault, or even the attempted murder of Jason Auch. And to top it all off, this megalomaniac once again made the critical decision to forgo formal legal representation by being his own attorney. Well, at least his sister returned to town for the show.

At the beginning of the month long trial Wassenaar spoke openly that he would have her (Lois) in "shreds" when he questions her about the rape allegations. But, once again, the man with a fool for a client was wrong; It seemed as though he forgot who he was dealing with; The Survivor Lois Fraley.

In the world of criminal justice it is practically unheard of when a rapist directly questions his victim about the details of the assault. The potential for intimidation aside, you would think that this self proclaimed "Legal Beagle" would realize that he is not going to gain any sympathy with a jury by grilling his victim.

Lois stayed strong and faced her predator openly in court. At one point of the trial Wassenaar did try to get dirty by attempting to rile this strong woman with the question, "Did you fear me when you came at me in The Tower?"

The determined correctional officer stood her ground by answering the convict's query directly, "Yes I did, very much so. I just finished seeing my partner slapped upside the head by a three-foot metal pole."

Wassenaar did not fair well by representing himself in

the courts of Arizona. Once again his plan to grandstand the jury with complaints of his mistreatment by the prison system was not received well.

It took the Maricopa County Superior Court jury less than five hours to all agree that Ricky K. Wassenaar a.k.a. "Rooster" was guilty of nineteen of the twenty counts that stemmed from the longest hostage siege in U.S. Prison history. As he stormed out of the courtroom escorted by officers, Ricky had to get the last word in by shouting, "Worst verdict I've ever seen in my life people."

And for him it was, Wassenaar was later sentenced for his role in the January 2004 hostage siege at ASPC-Lewis to more than 400 years in prison by Maricopa County Superior Court Judge Warren Granville. Sixteen of Wassenaar's nineteen convictions carry a life sentence. He will serve it consecutively, but only after finishing his current sentence for the Tucson robbery.

Kyla, now fifteen-years-old, has a better understanding of the woman who she has spent her entire life with. She has learned much about the adversity of her mother's early life as well as the hurdles that Lois has struggled with as a single parent working within a violent sector of society. Her better understanding came shortly after the release of the mother that she very easily could have lost forever.

In 2004 the young girl was kept in the dark about her mother's situation when early into the incident, she was swept away to a relatives home with the excuse and lie that Lois was working overtime. There she was sequestered from the nationwide media exposure at the State's recommendation.

When asked later about how Lois coped with reality during the siege, this woman who is a testament to survival, explains that she laughed, she joked, she cried, she prayed, she rocked while thinking of family, not only hers, but Jason's and Wassenaar's and Coy's.

She talked to her photos as if Tere and Kyla were with her, unfortunately several of those talks were ended with what even Lois thought might be her last goodbye, as the hostage pondered suicide.

Lois has survived her near fatal ordeal with a fresh perspective into the world that is her family. Shortly after her release Lois commented, "I had my family taken away, I had the moons and the stars and the suns all taken away."

So, how is The Survivor Lois Fraley doing now?

Just as you might expect, she is in recovery enduring and hopefully outliving the pain that these two malcontents have inflicted upon her psyche. She is strong, persistent, and will definitely carry on throughout her life to help others.

When dealing with the memories of the seige, she explains, "When times are really tough, I remind myself that I'm better off at this moment than I was when I was being held."

Lois also explains that she is being proactive in her own recovery by seeing a psychologist and a psychiatrist, and remaining on medications. She got a dog after her partner Tere complained about Lois talking to the plants, and then a speed bag and a heavy bag, which are normally used in boxing and martial arts.

But Lois' equipment is different than any that you will find in a gym or a spa. Her heavy bag wears a T-shirt that bears the images of Wassenaar and Coy. Even she will say, "I've got issues."

Since her release, her mettle has been tested several different times and has failed and succeeded in different ways. She stated, "I know that there can be a tendency to bury the memories and the feelings...I am very aware of the danger of doing that. So I keep setting goals for myself to cross new hurdles." These hurdles range from what some might consider minor, such as just putting her uniform back on, to what some may consider significant; a return to The Tower.

Several other hurdles included attending and testifying in both hostage takers' trials, as well as testifying in front of the Governor's Blue Ribbon Panel.

Her most recent hurdle is a lawsuit that was filed against her in Los Angeles County Superior Court in November, 2006. The suit was filed by a newsman who Lois trusted and credited with her survival after the siege, who convinced her to sign away the rights to her story; which until now has been held hostage for three years.

With the help of Robert Davis and Charles Hughes since her release, The Survivor Lois Fraley has been the inspiration for the creation of a 501 (c) (3) non-profit foundation with the intention of helping others to survive a critical incident.

Her heartfelt desire is to stand as a survivor providing inspiration as a beacon of light. She strongly supports the education of others by promoting the necessity of hostage survival training within high risk industries.

The proceeds of this book will help the Lois Fraley Foundation to achieve its worthwhile goals by helping those in need, and educating others.

 Glossary

Accommodation phase – The third, and longest phase of any hostage taking incident, when negotiators accommodate the hostage takers by bargaining for specified comfort items.

Admin – Short term for administration.

ADC – The Arizona Department of Corrections, also called ADC, the agency in charge of Arizona's prisons.

A.K.A. – Also known as. An alias.

Asps – Expandable metal batons used as truncheons.

Baton round – A less than lethal munition that projects skip-fire rounds.

Birdbaths – A method of bathing that inmates use when locked inside of their prison cells by washing their bodies from the small cell sink.

Bleeding out – A large flow of blood from an attack; usually a knife wound.

Blind Feeding – The system of feeding inmates their meals from behind a wall, not allowing access to the food handler.

Blue Yard – One of two designated recreation areas in the Morey Unit at the prison.

Breach – A gap made in a wall or fortification.

C/Os – Correctional Officers paid by the state to manage and protect the community from inmates within a prison by maintaining security and inmate accountability to prevent disturbances, assaults, and escapes.

Capstun – A brand of pepper gas spray also known as Oleorisincapsacum used to incapacitate violent inmates.

Cellie – Common prison term for cellmate or room mate.

Chimo – Prison jargon for a child molester. See also "Rapo."

Code-4 – Law enforcement term for "okay." Example: "Are you Code-4?"

Comfort items – Items provided by the negotiators to the hostage takers in order to attempt to end a situation peacefully. Comfort items include food, cigarettes and blankets.

Command – Short for Command Center, which is where the authoritative decision making takes place during a hostage incident.

Cutter – Someone who commits self mutilation by cutting themselves.

Dark Teams – Hostage Takers Wassenaar and Coy's terminology for Tactical Service Unit and Special Weapons and Tactics Team.

DPS – Arizona's Department of Public Safety

Dynamic Entry – The first phase of a hostage rescue, usually initiated with overpowering gunfire, violent force and a general disorientation for both hostage takers and hostages alike.

Fish – Prison jargon used by both inmates and officers to define inexperienced staff.

Food trap – A window used for the method of feeding inmates through a secure passage from the kitchen to the cafeteria.

Gator box – A secure sliding drawer that passes through one side of a wall to the other, similar to those seen in a bank.

Goon Squad – A prison term describing a special team of officers that are used for cell extractions and violent situations; fights, suicides, etc.

Graveyard Shift – Night Shift, specifically 8:40 PM to 6:40 AM.

Gurney – A flat table or stretcher with wheels for transporting patients during emergencies.

H/T – Hostage Taker

Hanger – Someone who attempts suicide by hanging themselves.

Hide – An area setup by a sniper and spotter, usually disguised.

Hot seat – The seat where the Primary Negotiator sits to communicate with the Hostage Takers.

IMS – Incident Management System. Arizona's alarm and response system for critical incidents occurring within ADC.

Jail House Lawyer – An inmate who does his own legal research and preparation for litigation.

Knee-knockers – Rubber or wooden less-than-lethal cylinders, also known as baton rounds, fired out of a 37 mm weapon.

Legal Beagle – A convict who is considered to be an expert in matters of law.

Less-than-lethal – A term used to describe weapons which are used to stop rather than kill. If aimed incorrectly these weapons can kill.

Lexan – Registered trademark of General Electric Company's polycarbonate resin thermoplastic, also known as bulletproof glass.

Lifer – An inmate serving a life sentence.

Lockdown – Confinement of a group of prisoners or an entire prison to their cells, usually in response to an emergency or unrest.

Med Call – Issuance of prescribed medications to offenders.

Military time – A method of timekeeping while sequentially using 24 hours, beginning at 0000 hours (Midnight) to 2359 (11:59 PM).

NOC – Negotiation Operation Center, where the Primary and Secondary Negotiators communicate with the hostage taker(s) in an effort to resolve the situation.

0 Dark 30 – A late night worker's term for early hours of their shift. See also "Graveyard Shift."

Orange Zone – A heightened state of alertness, with a specific "focal point."

Pat search - To search (a person) for concealed weapons, contraband goods, etc., through the person's clothing.

PS – Protective Segregation Inmate. PSs are isolated from the general population of a prison for security and safety concerns.

Pigs – Offender slang for any law enforcement officer- ranging from Correctional Officers to State Troopers.

Pigsticker – A prison made knife, usually created from makeshift objects. See also "shank," "shiv."

Pony – Prison Moniker for Steven Michael Coy, Inmate #047122.

Primary – The Primary Negotiator speaking with the hostage taker(s).

Rapo – A common term for a rapist. See also "chimo."

Red Yard – One of two designated recreation areas in the Morey Unit at the prison.

Red Zone – An alarmed state of awareness, commonly referred to as "Fight or Flight."

Resolution Phase – The final phase of any hostage incident which may end by peaceful resolution and surrender or a tactical hostage rescue. This is the second most dangerous phase.

Rooster – Ricky Kurt Wassenaar, Inmate #065155

SAU – Special Assignment Unit, which is the term for the Phoenix PD's full-time SWAT team.

Sack-of-nasties – Inmate term for sack lunches.

Sally Port – A secured entryway into and throughout a correctional facility.

Secondary – The Secondary Negotiator.

Shank – A prison made knife, usually created from makeshift objects. See also "pigsticker," "shiv."

Shiv – A prison made knife, usually created from makeshift objects. See also "pigsticker," "shank."

Simu shot – A well coordinated placement of sniper's shots on different targets simultaneously.

Sniper – A highly trained marksman.

Spotter – A member of a sniper team who assists the marksman by acquiring target pictures and discerning and disseminating critical information.

Sting ball grenade – A less-than-lethal rubber ball munition that disperses tear gas.

Stockholm Syndrome – A psychological phenomenon that occurs when a bond is formed between the hostage taker and the hostage, usually resulting from a mutual distrust for the authorities.

SWAT – Special Weapons and Tactics, a team of highly trained tactical officers.

Ten fifteen – Correctional designation for an inmate.

The Hole – A segregated area within a prison where inmates serve time in isolation for prison offenses.

Thorazine – Chlorpromazine, an anti-psychotic drug used primarily for the treatment of schizophrenia.

Tier – A row of prison cells in a cellblock.

"Type-A" Personality – A flat personality type with very strict tendencies and regimens.

TSU – The Department of Public Safety's Tactical Service Unit, similar to SWAT.

T-Zone – The primary target area for snipers consists of the forehead, brow and nose that will neutralize any target instantly.

Bibliography

"The Good Guys" Incident. April 4, 1991.
www.specwarnet.com/taclink/Ops/TheGoodGuys.htm

Freemen Surrender Peacefully to FBI. June 14, 1996.
www.cnn.com/US/9606/13/freemen.11p/

Transcript: American Morning, Interview with
Ivan Bartos. February 2, 2004.
cnnstudentnews.cnn.com/TRANSCRIPTS/0402/02/
ltm.10.html

Transcript: Interview of Correctional
Officer/ASPC-Lewis, Morey Unit.
Transcribed by Konetta Canfield, February 3, 2004.

Transcript of Governor's Advisory Blue Ribbon Panel.
Reported by Pamela J. Mayer,
Phoenix, Arizona, February 11, 2004.

Transcript of Governor's Advisory Blue Ribbon Panel.
Reported by Linda S. Christensen, Phoenix, Arizona,
February 12, 2004.

Transcript: 'This Ain't Acting Normal'.
February 13, 2004.
www.azcentral.com/news/articles/0213prison-hostagefe-male.html

Transcript: Hostage Obeyed 'Every Order'.
February 13, 2004.
www.azcentral.com/news/articles/0213prison-hostage-male13.html

Transcript of Governor's Advisory Blue Ribbon Panel.
Reported by Pamela J. Mayer,
Phoenix, Arizona, February 19, 2004.

Transcript of Officer Auch of the Governor's Advisory
Blue Ribbon Panel. Reported by Marcella L. Daughtry,
Phoenix, Arizona, February 26, 2004

Transcript of KTAR's Interview of the Female Hostage.
March, 2004, Phoenix, Arizona.

Preliminary Findings and Recommendations:
The Morey Unit Hostage Incident. Arizona
Department of Corrections, Phoenix, Arizona,
March 4, 2004.

In Their Own Words: The Kitchen Worker.
March 20, 2004.
www.azcentral.com/specials/special48/articles/
0319prison-transcript-ON.html

Arizona's Prison Boss. Jana Bommersbach, Feature
Story Phoenix Magazine,
December, 2004.

15 Days of Anguish. Dennis Wagner, Judi Villa, Amanda J. Crawford. The Arizona
Republic, 2004.

Anatomy of a Hostage Negotiation: An Interview with a
Primary Negotiator. John D. Baker,
The Negotiator Magazine, 2004.

Transcript of Anderson Cooper 360 Degrees,
May 5, 2005.
edition.cnn.com/TRANSCRIPTS/0505/05/acd.01/html

Transcription of interview provided by KTAR
February 2004.

Personal Interviews with Robert Davis. July 28 –
December 17, 2006. Keith Rapp Survival Resources.

About the Writers

Keith Rapp was employed by the Washington State Department of Corrections for seventeen years, gaining experience in dealing with Maximum Custody and Intensive Management Inmates. He worked directly with Protective Custody Inmates, Outpatient Mental Health Inmates. as well as Inmates Sentenced to the Death Penalty. He has remained with Condemned Inmates until the last moments of their lives as they have been walked to the gallows at the Washington State Penitentiary in Walla Walla, Washington.

Keith had a variety of duties within the Department of Corrections. He served as a Tactical Team Member of the Penitentiary's Emergency Response Team, he was as an instructor responsible for staff and officer training, as well as being active in workplace diversity matters. Teaching tolerance and acceptance is something that Keith loves to do.

As an instructor at The Correctional Officers Training Academy, he taught a wide variety of subjects with a focus on hostage negotiations and hostage survival. Keith is a certified Crisis/Hostage Negotiator and is considered a subject matter expert. He has been asked to travel throughout the state for speaking engagements. As a trainer and speaker, Keith has a dynamic presentation style that creates an interest in the subject matters he presents.

His recent interest in the fifteen day hostage standoff at the Arizona Prison Complex-Lewis has caused him to immerse himself into this critical incident, poring over

several hundreds of documents, transcripts, reports and recordings from this recent event. His original focus was to create a training vehicle for hostage survival and critical incident stress management for his hostage survival consulting service "Survival Resources." With the help of Robert Davis, Keith has added the human side of this epic story, along with the technical and the tactical aspects of this bureaucratic nightmare.
Please visit his website at
www.survivalresources.org

Robert Davis, Chairman of the Lois Fraley Foundation, holds an M.A. Degree in Counseling and Psychology specializing in the field of Human Behavior Analysis.

He is retired from the California Department of Corrections after eighteen years of service. During his career with the Department, he worked with Minimum to Maximum Security Inmates as a Correctional Peace Officer and completed his career as a Correctional Counselor.

His interest in the Arizona Prison Complex-Lewis hostage incident was due to his tenure as the Primary Negotiator for the California State Prison-Los Angeles County Crisis Response Team. He has completed extensive training in both Basic and Advanced Hostage Negotiator courses and is certified as a Crisis/Hostage Negotiator for the State of California.

He is a member of the California Association of Hostage Negotiators and has attended numerous classes, seminars, and conferences on Hostage Rescue and Survival. He has played a significant role in the peaceful resolution of many prison uprisings and critical incidents.
www.loisfraleyfoundation.com